MAKE IT

YOUR

BUSINESS

MAKE IT  YOUR BUSINESS

*The Definitive Guide
to Launching, Managing,
and Succeeding in
Your Own Business*

STEPHAN SCHIFFMAN

POCKET BOOKS
New York   London   Toronto   Sydney   Tokyo   Singapore

POCKET BOOKS, a division of Simon & Schuster Inc.
1230 Avenue of the Americas, New York, NY 10020

ISBN: 0-671-02178-8

First Pocket Books hardcover printing September 1998

10 9 8 7 6 5 4 3 2 1

POCKET and colophon are registered trademarks of
Simon & Schuster Inc.

Text design by Stanley S. Drate/Folio Graphics Co. Inc.

Printed in the U.S.A.

This, my twelfth book, is dedicated to my father,
Walter Leonard Schiffman.

CONTENTS

PART I **STARTING OUT** 1

1 Time for a Change: Working for Yourself 3

2 What It Takes 9

3 Your Financial Requirements 15

4 Ten Myths About Running Your Own Business 20

5 What Is Work to You? 28

6 The Seventy-five Percent Right Rule, or Failure and Success Revisited 31

7 The Pros and Cons of Starting From Scratch 36

8 Why You Are Always Your Own Best Salesperson 44

9 Handling Family Issues 49

PART II **BRANCHING OUT** 53

10 Your Most Important Asset: What You Focus On 55

11 Finding Your Business Niche 61

12 Thinking Your Way Through the First Year—and Beyond 65

13 Establishing Your Goals: The Art of Thinking Big 73

14 Reviewing What's Happening: Building Quiet
Time Into Your Day 77

15 Your Strategy Map 80

16 Getting a Fix on Your Ideal Customer 84

17 "Help! I Need Money." 88

18 "Help! I Need Good People." 97

19 "Help! I Need More Time." 104

20 Dealing With Attorneys (Yours or Someone Else's) 110

21 Dealing With Business Relationships That
Don't Work 114

PART III FINDING OUT 119

22 Marketing: Why People Buy 121

23 Customers Must Drive the Process 127

24 Going Directly to the Customer 133

25 The Advertising Agency Trap 138

26 The Daily-Call Routine 141

27 The Sales Cycle 154

28 Prospect Management Is Business Management 161

29 One on One 178

30 Second Meetings, Second Contacts 186

31 The Preliminary Proposal 191

32 Winning Commitment   196

33 Monitoring the Solutions You Deliver   201

PART IV GROWING UP   207

34 Managers: Being One, Hiring One   209

35 Why Growth Is Expensive   215

36 How to Handle a Market Crisis   222

37 Managing Your Business Over the Long Term   225

38 When the Business *Isn't* Performing the Way
You Want   229

39 When the Business *Is* Performing the Way You Want 233

40 Redefining Your Role   237

41 Selling Your Business   239

42 Successful Exit Strategies   245

Epilogue   249

Appendix A: Your Formal Business Plan   251

Appendix B: Interview Questions You Can Use
            to Evaluate Candidates for Employment   255

PART I

STARTING OUT

Make no mistake. Launching a business is hard work—when I launched mine, it was something close to an obsession for me. I took next to no time off, and I didn't see any real vacation time for a few years. I made quiet time for myself during the day, and I found a way to sneak in a weekend day with the family once in a while, but that was about it. That's not an uncommon experience.

Starting a business requires a certain amount of obsession. (It also helps to be very young, although that's not essential.) You have to be willing to put in one long day after another. You can't burn yourself out, but you can't treat this like your previous job, either. If you don't commit yourself fully to this enterprise, who will?

I believe that during your first year or two of business, you should probably plan on taking no vacation time. You're going into business—this is how you're going to make your livelihood. When people start a business, I usually recommend to them that they completely commit to it and spend two full years understanding the choices that they've made. If your choice to become more successful and to own your own business is going to pay off for you, you will need to be totally "invested" in the proposition, just as I was.

1

TIME FOR A CHANGE: WORKING FOR YOURSELF

So you want to work for yourself.

Why? Did you wake up one day and know at once that it was time to make this change, or did you agonize over it for a long time before coming to a cautious decision? What motivated you to pick up this book?

Some people wake up in the middle of the night with a great commercial idea, one they believe will be a big seller and make them a millionaire. Other people are simply tired of the comfortable routine of their nine-to-five job and are eager to take some risks. Still others are dissatisfied with the hierarchy and lines of authority they associate with their own current working conditions and are eager to call their own shots. Perhaps you want more freedom to do what you want to do and to gain a real sense of satisfaction from your own work. Or perhaps other circumstances have dictated your decision to start working for yourself. Maybe you were laid off from your job and decided now was the time to see what you could do on your own. It could be you have a particular talent that you want to exploit, perhaps a technical expertise in some area, and this has led to your conception of a new business possibility. Or is there another reason you've decided to consider entering the world of the entrepreneur?

Here's another important question: *What do you expect?* Are you anticipating that you will be immersed in your work for hours, weeks, and years on end—in other words, do you thrive on challenges? Or is your goal to get the business launched and then fly off to Tahiti to relax while the underlings run everything for you?

Well, whatever your reasons for making this big change and whatever you hope to get out of it, you should closely examine its pros and cons before taking the plunge into self-employment and entrepreneurship. You have to know—thoroughly—both the advantages and the disadvantages of calling your own shots so that you can go into this venture with your eyes wide open. You must be willing to accept both the peaks and the valleys of what lies ahead of you. Smart entrepreneurs that I've spoken to know there is more to be gained from the whole process than large sums of money or influence. Even if you never become the next Bill Gates, there is still plenty of satisfaction to be found in owning and operating your own business, especially if you score a hit with the product or service you'll be offering.

First and foremost, there is your idea. It's all yours—nobody else's. Whether it's a product, a service, or a solution, your idea must be exciting to you if it's going to get you into business on your own. (In fact, if you are truly going to succeed, your idea has to be nothing short of great!) And because it's your idea, you care about it the way you have cared about no other job that entailed working for somebody else. This can be highly motivating, and very energizing. The most successful small-business owners I've known have been those who have willingly and eagerly accepted the long hours and sacrifices that went with getting their business off the ground, simply because it was their business—their baby, if you will. When you truly care about something, you will do whatever it takes to *make it your business.*

That means tending your dream, nurturing it, helping it to grow. Your total involvement in your work will motivate you like nothing else ever has, and that can be a very satisfying feeling!

Running a business yourself also allows you to utilize more of your talents than you ordinarily would in a "regular" job. Rather than being constricted by a specific job description written by somebody in the human resources department, you can set out your job description as you see fit. All those ideas you have had all these years about how you'd run things if you were in charge can now be put to good and satisfying use. You can do things according to your own lights and without the fear of stepping on other people's toes or doing something that runs afoul of some obscure policy manual. You write the rules now! And that makes it possible for you to become involved in all the different areas of the business you're starting, which can be both challenging and stimulating for you—and daunting, as well.

One of the downsides to being in charge is that you have to do things you may not be very good at doing, or have a distaste for. Paperwork, for instance. If you thought you had lots of paperwork when you worked for somebody else, just wait until you start doing it all on your own! Either you'll get really good at filling out tax forms, or you'll have an ongoing relationship with your accountant, which, I will happily confess, is my method. For many that I know, paperwork is the bane of their existence. Others find ways to handle all the formal reporting obligations and still focus on the tasks that really interest them. Beyond suggesting that you find a good accountant, I would strongly advise you to follow a simple piece of advice that many beginning entrepreneurs ignore to their peril: Never ignore correspondence from the Internal Revenue Service! (It's easier to do than you may think.)

There may be other areas that will slow you down in the beginning. For instance, you may not be a financial whiz and will need to seek assistance in handling the monetary aspects of your start-up venture. Or maybe one of your employees isn't working out and for the first time in your life you are faced with the task of having to fire somebody—a tough job. Being an entrepreneur also means that "doing your best" sometimes isn't good enough. When you were an employee and things got difficult, you could give a problem your "best effort" and perhaps pass it along to someone else if things didn't work out. When you run your own business, the ultimate responsibility for resolving a problem always resides with you. When a key employee gets sick or a critical piece of equipment breaks down or a manufacturer reports an unexpected delay, you're the one who has to come up with a solution. (Remember that sign Harry Truman used to keep on his desk: "The Buck Stops Here.")

This is not to say that you yourself have to be able to resolve every detail of every problem. But you do have to know how to get the help you need when you need it, and you have to be willing to follow up to make sure things are completed properly. You'll need other people to help you get over the rough spots in the early stages—and believe me, there will be rough spots!—as well as to provide a network that you can use to your advantage as your company grows. You'll need to learn the art of delegating—identifying key goals and entrusting them to someone else whose methods you believe (with cause!) will be as effective and responsible as your own. At the end of the day, however, the responsibility will be yours.

So, when you're in charge, you're the one who determines the direction the company takes and provides the goals and the focus for your employees. You write the company's mission statement, you create the policies, you do the hiring, you oversee the finances, you solve the crises. In other words—you do it all! You must be prepared for the advantages and disadvantages that come with this commitment, including, in all likelihood, occasional long hours and occasional sleepless nights. Your workweek will sometimes seem endless—eight days a week, as the old song has it. You will be living and breathing your business day in and day out. It will follow you wherever you go, even when you think you've left everything at the office. If you're running the business out of your home, then it will always seem to be beckoning to you, even when you're trying to take some time off. If there's a serious crunch on to get your product out the door or a crucial deal that's on the verge of being closed or a crisis that's in the process of being resolved, you may find yourself continuously on the phone and up late every night, even when you have employees who are running interference for you. The fact is, your business is your baby in a sense, and you must always be monitoring it and making sure it's well, right down to changing the diapers—especially when your baby is still an infant.

Understandably, starting up a business will probably change your life entirely, and that includes your personal relationships. You need to be prepared for the high moments and the possible pitfalls, and the personal aspect may be the most important element to consider, especially if yours is a family business. Not only can personal disputes in a family-owned operation destroy relationships, they can also interrupt your company's productivity and possibly bring it down altogether.

Your business is there to bring you many rewards—but it will bring many headaches as well. On the plus side, the profits you earn are yours. On the minus side, any liability and losses are also yours. Another plus: You can set your own salary. Another minus: You may need to sacrifice a portion of your salary to keep the business going. A plus: You have the latitude to apply creative solutions to problems. A minus: There's only yourself to blame if your solutions don't work.

As you can see, for every advantage you may have as an owner of your own business, there is a potential disadvantage—one for which you must be prepared. My own experience is that, if you make the plusses work for you, the minuses tend to diminish in importance.

Success starts with a positive attitude, and that means having confidence in yourself and believing in your own ability to make it all work. That's your first big advantage—attitude. By maintaining a positive outlook, by believing in the idea that forms the basis for your company, and by giving it your best shot, you have already put yourself well on the road to success.

To help maintain that positive attitude, periodically remind yourself of the many, many advantages you have gained by employing yourself: control; creativity; the chance to put your talents to good use; the opportunity to do it all; total involvement in work that you enjoy; an atmosphere where your input is always appreciated; a way to make something exciting happen; self-fulfillment; being able to prove what you can do; profits and other monetary rewards (if not immediately, then down the road); and so on.

As for the disadvantages, you'll need to be aware of what they are and develop strategies for dealing with them. (That's where this book will help.) If the line of work you've chosen is for you, you'll learn to anticipate the difficult elements, and you'll learn to develop coping techniques that will get you through the rough spots.

It should go without saying that you must be prepared to work hard—especially in the early period. What lies ahead of you involves a great deal of effort—effort that's only worth your attention if you truly love doing what you do all day long. With that kind of love and with the right attitude, you can turn even a disadvantage to your advantage. That's because for some people—and perhaps for you—*making it your own business* is the only lifestyle that really makes sense.

In the next chapter, we'll talk about how you can determine whether you're ready for the demands of getting your own business up and running.

2

WHAT IT TAKES

Here's a thought: In 1996 more than eight hundred thousand new independent businesses were launched. Only about thirty percent of those businesses have survived to the present day, and an even smaller percentage have made it into the multimillion-dollar bracket. So the odds will be against you when you start out—unless you ask yourself the right questions.

How do you know you have what it takes to launch and then operate your own business? Here are some of the most important questions you will need to ask yourself. If you develop realistic answers to each of the ten questions that follow, you'll be well positioned to take advantage of the information in this book.

1. Do You Have Something Customers Are Willing to Pay For? My own personal opinion is that if the customers are there, just about any other hurdle can be overcome. You can start a business without much money, you can pick up what you need to know as you go along about operations and shipping, you can find a tax expert to help you handle the paperwork . . . but if you're trying to sell something for which there is no market, your business is doomed. Too many first-time entrepreneurs get sidetracked on questions that have nothing to do with keeping customers happy. What will the decor of the office look like? (If your customers never see it, who cares?) What can Uncle Harold do around the office? (If he isn't helping you to win customers or to keep them happy, his place on the payroll is suspect.) Where should we go to buy office supplies? (If you can't resolve a question like that quickly and efficiently, you're wasting time that you could be devoting to your customers.) Ask yourself, How will my company make people's lives easier—and what makes me think they'll pay for that? Are you offering your customers a *product*—a new type of windshield wiper that lasts fifty percent longer than anything else that's on the market now? Are you offering them a *service*—an evaluation of their manufacturing plant's ability to pass a stringent environmental inspection, or recommendations on how to meet government requirements governing plant emissions? Do you offer a combination of a product and a service—say, by selling your customer a copier and then signing him or her up for a repair contract good for the following five years? If you can't answer questions like these, you're not ready to start planning your business.

   2. Who Else Is Offering What You Plan to Offer? If you don't have at least a basic idea of the business your competitors conduct—how they reach customers, what kinds of customers they reach, what the advantages and disadvantages of their products and services are—then you'll be operating in the dark. Your own work experience should have given you some idea of what's out there. You should expand on this by following events in the industry you wish to enter, perhaps by taking a look at the relevant trade magazines available in your local library. When in doubt, ask the reference librarian—for example, "Who makes widgets for the agricultural products industry?"

3. What "Intellectual Capital" Do You Bring to the Table? Your own technical expertise or working knowledge is another factor to consider. Just as important is your sense of passion and enjoyment for the work you do. Just because you're good at something doesn't mean you want to spend twelve hours a day doing it. (I can type—but I don't like typing all day long, so I shouldn't start a typing business!) If your business is based on something you really enjoy and are exceptionally good at doing, you'll be more likely to succeed.

4. Do You Believe in What You're Doing? Do you have a sense of mission about this undertaking? If not, don't bother. Are you confident enough in both your idea and yourself to get the job done? If so, this will be one of your biggest assets. Your faith in your product or service is what will enable you to be effective in your dealings with other people. If you're starting out on this venture all alone, without partners or employees, your attitude becomes especially important, as you must be all things to all people at all levels. You are chairman of the board, middle management, and slave labor all rolled into one hardworking package, and you have to have the confidence in yourself to handle all the different tasks that must be attended to in order to get the job done. If you can't assert yourself, then you will come across as weak and ineffective. But beware of being too assertive! This may be viewed as arrogance, which will work against you.

5. Do You Know When to Ask for Help? "I've got it all figured out!" Do you? I've known many an entrepreneur who was doomed to failure from the start because he or she plunged into the new venture without ever getting any form of counsel from wiser heads. As much as you may think you can do it all, the fact is, you have to utilize as many resources as you can and educate yourself as thoroughly as you can. Nobody can handle everything. You must be ready to ask people for advice, and you must also be willing to develop relationships with key people who can help you fill in your blind spots. For instance, if you have no experience whatsoever in managing people and your business is intensely staff-driven, it will behoove you to either learn what makes for good staffing and managerial decisions or hook up with someone who's got more experience in this area than you do. (Appendix B contains some of the best questions to ask applicants during face-to-face interviews.)

6. Can You Work on Your Own? Some people simply need a boss in order to be motivated to get work done. You must be ruthlessly honest with yourself on this score. Monitor your own work closely. If you find that your most productive days are always those when someone else is dictating what you should do next, and that days when you operate on your own are days when nothing much happens, there's a problem. You're probably not cut out to be an entrepreneur. You should think seriously about staying in a work environment that allows you to make contributions to an existing organization.

7. Can You Prioritize Your Day Effectively? If you're like most beginning entrepreneurs, you won't be able to afford a lot of administrative help in the early stages. Without the ability to organize and prioritize your work, you may find yourself in a maze of lost papers, missed deadlines, and ticked-off customers. But remember, entrepreneurship means knowing how to get things done—even when you yourself can't do them. If you are one of those people who can't organize his or her way out of a paper bag, your plan should incorporate adequate administrative support to keep your company running smoothly. If such support is not possible in the beginning, then you will definitely need to strategize how you are going to keep you and your workload organized well enough to stay out of the soup until you can afford that support.

8. Do You Have a High Energy Level? As you should know by now, starting a new business requires long, countless hours of hard work and an incredible amount of mental toughness. This means you have to have the energy and the stamina to stick it out through thick and thin. How healthy are you? Any physical or mental ailments will sap your strength and deplete your energy. If you are not able to devote yourself one hundred percent to your efforts, you will need to consider the effect this will have on your ability to stay on top of what will be a highly demanding workload.

9. Can You Keep Setbacks and Rejection in Perspective? There will be days when you'll be exhausted and perhaps even down periods when the temptation to quit may be strong. Will you treat these as "bumps in the road"—or judgments against you as a person? There will be circumstances you didn't anticipate or an unfortunate calamity in the market that will directly affect your product or service. Whatever form the downslide might take, the question is, How will you react to it? The most successful entrepreneurs I've known are those who kept going, who didn't let the occasional setback bring them down altogether but kept working away with an upbeat, tenacious attitude. I've also known unsuccessful business owners who allow the least little thing to get them down, time and again. They obsess about the details and fail to see the big picture of what they're trying to accomplish. Details are important—but so is keeping a levelheaded attitude. You have to keep working at your goals, no matter how many distractions and obstacles are placed in your path!

10. Are You Ready to Motivate Yourself? Frustration and fatigue will be your frequent companions, and you may occasionally lose the motivation that got you started in the first place. If your loss of motivation persists for a lengthy period of time, you may need to take a good, long look at what you're doing and evaluate whether it's worthwhile to continue. So ask yourself if you are absolutely sure that you can sustain your motivation through all the downs, as well as the ups. You may find it helpful to periodically review all the reasons why you went into business for yourself in the first place. One entrepreneur I know made a written list of all the factors that motivated her to start working for herself. She keeps that list posted over her desk and reads it often. Sometimes she is even inspired by a new motivation, which she adds to the list. Knowing why you're doing what you're doing is the key to maintaining your determination to succeed. Think of it this way: When you start out, there's a fire inside you. You have to stoke that fire all the time and keep it burning continuously in order to have the energy you need to keep going. You're like a locomotive, heading to a particular destination. If you don't keep stoking the fire, the train will stop dead on the tracks and you'll never get to where you want to be.

How Did You Do?

I believe that not everyone is cut out to be an entrepreneur. If only one of your answers to the preceding questions came out "wrong," you should know that there's a very good chance that you are not well positioned to start or run a business. If two or more of your answers fall into this category, you are definitely making a mistake by trying to launch your own enterprise. And if you do not yet have a satisfactory answer to question one—which concerns the product or service you offer—you are definitely not ready to enter the world of entrepreneurship.

Being a successful entrepreneur means having "true grit." You need to be an expert in many areas and to have resources to draw on in other areas. You need stamina, good health, courage, determination, motivation, good judgment, analytical skills, leadership abilities, assertiveness, knowledge, and a willingness to take risks. You need to be a bit of an improvisationalist, too—to be able to come up with creative solutions when the standard ones just won't do the trick. Most of all, you've got to have the motivation, self-confidence, and mental toughness to press on in the face of sometimes overwhelming odds.

3

YOUR FINANCIAL
REQUIREMENTS

Some people feel they're not ready to start up a business until they have "enough money saved up," a process that can sometimes take years. Others plunge into the world of entrepreneurship without so much as a thought for how they'll make ends meet while they're getting things off the launching pad. Both choices represent serious errors in strategy.

Your personal financial situation is unique and should be addressed in concert with a financial planner or other qualified professional. You will have to know how much money you're going to need to get your business launched and to keep it going until it begins to support itself. There are two areas you will need to consider, business expenses and personal expenses.

How much is it going to cost you to get your business started? Set up an expense chart in which you list every item you will need to purchase and every expenditure you will need to make to get your business off the ground. Omit no

details, however slight they may seem to you: office furniture
and equipment, rent, utilities and telephone, supplies, inventory, fees, legal and accounting services, manufacturing
costs, marketing, advertising and promotions, and so on.
With each item on your list, write down an estimate of how
much money you're going to need within the amount of time
specified for your start-up. You'll find an example of such a
chart in Exhibit 1. If you don't have all the information yet,
rest assured that you're in very good company. (Part of entrepreneurship is making the best decisions you can, given the
information you have at your disposal!) Yes, important questions about, for instance, pricing and marketing may still not
have been addressed in detail. For now, make your best first-
draft estimates conservative ones. Your aim is to determine
how *much* you will need to keep afloat, not how little. For
help in developing working figures that will help you make
the best decisions at this early stage, speak to a trusted colleague or counselor. (See Appendix A for information on con-
tacting the Small Business Administration.)

Of course, you will also have to estimate what you're going
to need for your own living expenses. Traditional wisdom
holds that you should have up to twelve months' worth of
savings to live on. However, this number can vary depending
on the type of business you have, what you expect your income to be, and how soon you expect to start making money
from the business. (*Warning:* The date when you will begin to
turn a profit is almost certainly farther off than you think it
will be!) If you feel that you won't have enough to live on and
run your business, you may want to consider an alternative
source of income—a part-time job, or freelance work, for example—that will get you by until you get your business up
and running. (Remember what we said earlier about the importance of high daily energy levels?)

Just as you did for your business, you will need to calculate
just how much you're going to need to live on. Once again,
put together an expense chart that calculates what you'll need
for your mortgage or rent, groceries and supplies, loan and

EXHIBIT 1

Assessing Your Monthly Cash Requirements

Develop monthly estimates in each of the following categories:

A. OFFICE NEEDS
   1. Rent of office space _____
   2. Furniture (lease or purchase) _____
   3. Photocopy/fax machines (lease or purchase) _____
   4. Computer/printer _____
   5. Telephone/modem _____
   6. Heat/electricity _____
   7. Basic supplies (pens, pencils, paper, desk accessories, etc.) _____
   8. Company letterhead/business cards _____
   9. Postage, shipping services _____

B. STAFFING
   1. Owner's salary _____
   2. Employee payroll _____
   3. Benefits (health insurance, workers' compensation, etc.) _____
   4. Tax contributions (FICA, Social Security, etc.) _____

C. SERVICES
   1. Accountant _____
   2. Attorney _____
   3. Temporary staffing solutions _____
   4. Subcontractors _____

D. MANUFACTURING
   1. Product development costs (samples, etc.) _____
   2. Lease of factory or other production space _____
   3. Lease/purchase of manufacturing equipment/machinery _____
   4. Supplies/raw materials _____
   5. Labor _____
   6. Inventory start-up _____

E. DISTRIBUTION
   1. Packaging _____
   2. Shipping costs _____

F. MARKETING
   1. Advertising/publicity (production costs and media charges) _____
   2. Special offers/promotions _____
   3. Sales literature/brochures (design and production) _____
   4. Mailing list rental _____
   5. Postage for mailings/publicity _____
   6. Client entertainment _____

G. OTHER COSTS
   1. Permits/fees/registrations _____
   2. Licenses _____
   3. Taxes _____
   4. Insurance (property, liability, auto or truck, errors and omissions) _____
   5. Signs _____
   6. Transportation (business automobile/truck) _____
   7. Subscriptions/memberships to professional journals/ organizations _____

---

credit card payments, taxes, insurance, monthly bills, utilities, entertainment, home maintenance, education, and so forth. Figure this into your overall calculations as you determine how much you're going to need altogether for both your business and your personal life. Your final estimate should have a built-in safety net. Figure in an extra fifteen percent to cover unanticipated expenses. See chart in Exhibit 2.

As you calculate what you're going to need for yourself and your start-up, versus what you already have, this will tell you whether it will be necessary to apply for a loan. If it is necessary, you should have two things to back you up: a good credit history and collateral of some sort. (If your business is

EXHIBIT 2

Determining Your Personal Assets and Liabilities

Assets

House or condominium _____
Property _____
Automobile _____
Furniture/antiques _____
Family heirlooms _____
Jewelry _____
Insurance policy(ies) _____
Bank account(s) _____
Trust fund(s) _____
Stocks/bonds/investments _____
IRA _____

Liabilities

Rent/mortgage _____
Credit card debt _____
Loan payments _____
Insurance payments _____
Personal expenses _____

one that does not involve inventory—if, for instance, you're thinking about starting a consulting firm—you should know during this early planning stage that banks will not be enthusiastic about loaning money without "hard" collateral. You may need to find alternate financing sources. See Chapter 17 for more information and ideas on this score.)

You'll begin to make a profit when your income exceeds your outgo—that's when your business will start paying for itself and funds will be available internally to expand and improve your operations (or, who knows, to pay you a bonus). Until that magic moment, you have to ensure that you can stay afloat, and that means doing careful planning and preparation.

To repeat: *Be Conservative!* It's far better to wait a month or two to develop a sound financial plan—one that ensures your own personal income—than to find yourself in the middle of a financial crisis halfway through your first year.

TEN MYTHS ABOUT RUNNING YOUR OWN BUSINESS

As you get started on your path to self-employment, you're going to receive a lot of advice, both solicited and unsolicited, about what you're letting yourself in for and what to expect as you go along. A great deal of what you hear will have some basis in fact, but a lot of it will also be based on a mythology that over the years has grown around small-business culture. The shame of it is that a great many people are enticed to make the plunge into self-employment by the belief that these myths are true, only to learn too late that they've been hornswoggled. Therefore, before you take that plunge, let's examine and debunk the ten most popular myths you're likely to encounter.

MYTH 1

I'm free! I no longer have a boss!

Not only do you have to account to yourself, you now have dozens and dozens—or perhaps hundreds or thousands—of

people to report to. They're called customers. There's no getting around it: Your clients will boss you around as no employer ever did. They will be more demanding and more
nitpicky and will place more expectations on you than you
ever dreamed possible. Your attention to their needs will be
paramount in your work. So just when you thought you had
broken free of the bonds of servitude, you will in many ways
find those bonds tighter than ever.

And let's not forget your responsibility to yourself! As your
own boss, you have to monitor yourself constantly—and
often you're going to be harder on yourself than your old boss
ever was. You will, in fact, find working for yourself is a lot
tougher than working for somebody else was. It requires
greater discipline, greater results, and a greater sense of responsibility.

MYTH 2

*There are more advantages to working for myself than working
for somebody else.*

Humbug. This is true only for a small percentage of the popu-
lation who genuinely feel confined in a structured situation.
It's a fact that some people just weren't meant for an office
environment. Taking risks and living on the edge—which is
what is entailed in owning your own business—gives them a
sense of fulfillment greater than anything they could accomplish in a cubicle.

But for most of us, the fact is that we like structure more
than we are willing to admit. Sure, we may chafe at the feeling of servitude we experience in having to report to somebody else and account for our actions, not to mention having
to do tasks that may be odious to us. But we are also working
in an environment that has a built-in safety net. We have a
guaranteed salary and comfortable benefits. We interact with
other people who, in many cases, become like a second family to us. If we work in middle management, we are removed

from many of the big crises and tough decisions that the top executives have to make. For many of us, the structure of our jobs keeps us in line and enables us to stay focused on what we have to do.

When you're on your own, you have to determine your hours, you have to solve the crises, you have to perform incredible feats of juggling, and you have to do this without allowing yourself to be distracted by the many temptations you now have access to (for example, taking a break to watch that certain television program). Having to do it all can be positively overwhelming at times, despite the thrills and challenges. Working for somebody else is safe and comfortable. Working for yourself is a risky adventure filled with surprises and pitfalls. If you choose the adventure, just remember: It won't be a bed of roses!

MYTH 3

At last! I can work only when I feel like it.

Want to bet? You'll find it was a lot simpler when you were able to go into the office, do what was expected of you, and go home again. You're in a whole new ball game now, one where you're continuously at bat. If you want your business to succeed, you'll be requiring yourself to put in long hours— and they will include most of those times when you don't feel like working.

If you're going to pick and choose the times when you will or will not work at your business, then be prepared for cash problems. Refusing to work just because the spirit is unwilling on a particular day could bring about a missed deadline, which will in turn generate an unhappy customer, which may result in lost revenues for you.

If anything, you now have to work harder than you ever did. I've already stressed the need for you to put in long, arduous hours at your job. There's a reason for that. You have to accept the fact that working for yourself is a whole lot harder than working for somebody else. The prospect of determining your own schedule may seem like paradise to you, but the demands of your business will make that kind of self-determination virtually impossible.

This brings us to . . .

MYTH 4

I'll have more time for myself, my spouse, my kids, whatever.

Wrong, wrong, wrong. If anything, you'll have less time and will find yourself performing a juggling act to keep the personal and professional demands on your time as balanced as possible.

What if you're working out of your home? You will need to take extra care not to let familial and other distractions eat into the time you need to devote to your business. The same pitfall lies here as in the myth of thinking you can control your own schedule. The more time you spend on other pursuits and the less time you give to running your business, the more likely you are to lose customers—and profits.

MYTH 5

I don't need other people. I can do it all myself.

We've already briefly examined this issue. Unless you're Superman or Superwoman, this is extremely unlikely. You can't possibly know it all, and you can't possibly have had adequate experience in virtually every aspect of running a business to make it a success. You may be inept with numbers or be faced with legal ramifications you hadn't considered or have to deal with new technologies for which you have no training. No matter how strong you are in certain areas, there will always be some aspect of the business in which you are weak. Many people conclude—with some impressive evidence on their side—that the safest bet is to start out with a partner who can cover their weak spots and enable them to concentrate on their strengths. In other words, if you're planning to start an advertising agency, you may want to consider an arrangement under which one person (say, you) is the "creative" partner, while the other is the "numbers" partner.

You may also find yourself with a business that has unexpectedly (and fortuitously) skyrocketed, leaving you with even less time than you had before because of all the orders you have to fill. You have to have help, or you won't be able to meet your obligations. This means hiring and then managing employees—another area for which you may be unprepared.

The fact is, people always need other people if they expect to survive and to cope with all they have to do. You may think it's a sign of weakness to ask others for help or advice—in either the short or long term. Not true! It's a sign of strength when you know how to take advantage of external resources and where to go to get the type of the assistance you need. You may think that having a partner or hiring employees (perhaps on a temporary basis) will eat into your profit margin, but in fact with proper support in key areas, your business is more likely to grow and generate even greater revenues.

Most important of all, having adequate support from a partner and/or key employees means being able to preserve both your health and your sanity. Trying to do everything will only put an enormous stress on your physical and mental resources that will do you and the company no good. So be smart: Don't do it alone!

MYTH 6

I've built a better mousetrap! Now the world is going to beat a path to my door.

Without proper marketing and a whole lot of attention to detail, great ideas often go nowhere. You may have the right idea at the right time, but simply having that "better mouse-trap" isn't enough. You have to find a way to get customers to connect to it! Ideas alone don't make the sales.

The best way to turn a good idea into a financial success is good old-fashioned one-on-one personal marketing on the part of the entrepreneur. We'll be talking about that in much greater detail later on in the book.

MYTH 7

I can undercut my competitors' price and lure away their customers.

First of all, one of your initial concerns in starting up a business is ensuring that production costs are not going to break you. If you intend to price your product or service fairly low, then you'd better make certain that you produce it at a low enough cost to gain you a reasonable profit. Just because you're starting small doesn't mean you can or should be beating the competition on price. In fact, it's a very good bet that your best option is to aim for the high-end customer who is willing to pay a higher price for a better product.

Many people equate price with quality. If your prices are too low, this will cause some customers to doubt the quality of what you have to offer. And if you end up committing to a price that doesn't make economic sense for your business, you may end up with far more unhappy customers than happy ones.

MYTH 8

I can call my own shots from now on.

Sure—sometimes. But more often than not, you'll be finding a lot of other people calling the shots for you. You may start out your day with a list of what you aim to accomplish, but by day's end, you'll be surprised at how few items have been ticked off. Once that phone starts ringing, somebody is bound to start changing your plans and making it necessary for you to adjust and readjust as the day goes along. Your shots will be dictated by the customer who wants his order shipped immediately or the sale is lost; or by the supplier who has failed to deliver on a promise, which affects promises you made to others; or by the employee who quits unexpectedly, leaving you holding the bag; or by the partner who made a crucial decision without consulting you.

There will always be others who have a say, either directly or indirectly, in what you do and how you do it. The idea that you'll be able to call the shots is more fantasy than reality. You can only control events as best you can.

MYTH 9

I need a written plan only if I'm trying to raise money.

Wrong again! A written plan is much more than something you choose to put together for the benefit of potential investors. It's a road map of the future of your company. It states what your company is all about—how it's going to be organized; how you are going to price, sell, and distribute your product; where your money will come from; how it will be spent; and the qualifications of those who will be running the company. A good plan is the backbone of your company, and it deserves to be put on paper. It provides the necessary structure and support to keep you on track to meet your goals.

Consider, too, that you never know when you're going to need to borrow money! You may think you have enough to get started, but what happens if initial sales don't meet your expectations and you suddenly find yourself short of cash? It may then become necessary to raise capital, in which case you'd better have a plan ready to adapt to the bank's requirements—just in case.

We'll be talking about the best ways to set your goals on paper later on in this book.

MYTH 10

Life will be simpler if I work for myself.

Running a business can be exhilarating, frustrating, energizing, maddening, supremely satisfying, and any number of other things—but it's not simple. In the early stages, especially, there may well be bigger worries, increased stress, and more pressure than you have ever known before.

Sure, there are plenty of hassles involved in working for somebody else. But as has already been mentioned, there is also a structure and security to be found in outside employment, going to work each day knowing what is expected of you and then getting it done, even if you find that job boring or stifling. Many new entrepreneurs talk about how they look forward to "unpredictability" or a "change of pace" in their jobs, but overlook that these sudden shifts can be very challenging indeed.

Your personal life will also be complicated. A meeting with a client may go on for so long that you're unable to make your daughter's school play. Or you may go for days at a time without seeing your family. Or you may repeatedly cancel dates because of a series of mishaps at the office. Or you may find yourself screaming at your loved ones because they're making noise when you're trying to work. The demands your business places on you also require that those who love and care about you be understanding and accommodating of you and your harried schedule—something that is not always easy for them or for you. So never expect life to be any simpler. There are complications you haven't even thought of yet!

5

WHAT IS WORK TO YOU?

Why bother putting all this time, effort, and energy into your business?

You should have a direct, motivating answer to that question. The most important thing you will have going for you as you start up a new business is yourself. You are your biggest asset. That means that the reasons you use to "stoke your own engine" must be good ones. So what does this work mean to you? What are you *committed* to doing? Not just *interested* in doing, but *committed* to doing? If your answer to those questions doesn't leave you feeling better about yourself and your efforts, you need to keep asking them until you come up with something that does.

Your own idea is what got you started in this direction, and the drive and determination within you must keep you going. So make sure that you're ready for the challenge by determining exactly what you expect of yourself and your business and making sure it means something powerful to you.

In this book, we'll be talking a lot about goal setting and vision and the ways you can mentally prepare yourself for the challenges of running a business. But all of that advice is worth nothing if your work has no real meaning for you.

In other words, you have to make your company your business—not your hobby! That means it gets all the dedication, effort, and attention you can possibly muster, because its goals are ones that get your juices flowing.

If you haven't already thought about it, now is the time to consider your personal motivation for starting your business. It could be humanitarian: You have thought of something that will be of tremendous medical or scientific value to people, and you want to get it out there so that it will provide its benefits immediately. Or it could be material: You simply want to make a great deal of money so that you can, for instance, provide your family with the very best. Or perhaps your goal is highly personal: You get a thrill out of taking risks and you thrive in an intense, hard-paced environment.

Whatever your motivation for working, make sure it translates into a *mission*.

Take a moment now, before you move ahead in this book, to write your personal and organizational mission—the reason you are committing to work as hard on your business as you'll be working. Your mission might look like any of these examples:

- *For someone with a love of making others happy:* I am committed to developing quality recreational products for elderly people.
- *For someone who has had a lifelong love affair with both flying and computer programming:* I am committed to producing the most advanced air-traffic-control software available.
- *For someone who loves to teach and to speak publicly:* I am committed to providing superior sales-training service to corporate clients—and thereby dramatically increasing their profitability and overall performance.

- *For partners with extensive backgrounds in preventive maintenance:* We are committed to developing the finest industrial maintenance equipment for our customers—and to helping them resolve their maintenance problems easily and quickly.

Make sure your mission, your commitment, is broad enough to address the passion that brought you into the business in the first place—and specific enough to help you evaluate whether or not new initiatives match up with your basic motivations for starting your business.

If the commitment you put down on paper doesn't *automatically* remind you, on a visceral level, why you decided to start your own business, you're not done working on it yet!

6

THE SEVENTY-FIVE PERCENT
RIGHT RULE, OR FAILURE AND
SUCCESS REVISITED

People who have spent a significant amount of time working for others sometimes get sidetracked by the idea of doing work "correctly" or "right" in their own business. They focus less than they should on their gut beliefs—and more than they should on what various outside "experts" think. It's a shame. People who run their own businesses need to learn to follow their own instincts about what is and isn't right—and they need to become comfortable with the possibility that, some of the time, they're going to make mistakes—just as the "experts" are going to.

When I talk to new business proprietors who are used to reporting to others, I usually find that for them words like "right" or "correct" have one particular meaning. All too often, it's "authorized." This idea usually comes out of one's experience in dealing with superiors. If a report has been submitted to a superior for authorization and has won that approval or received feedback that equals approval, then the report was "right." It was free of disapproval. It was therefore good.

That's the way lots of people in the working world look at what they do all day long. They ask themselves, "What do I have to do to get Ms. Bigshot to approve this?"

The problems arise when these people try to move from being a subordinate to being an entrepreneur. They often make a classic beginner's mistake. In applying standards to the work they do, they talk about "attention to detail" or "wanting to get it all right," but the end result is that they get confused and completely bogged down. They look for a superior to approve whatever they've just developed, without regard to whether or not the "expert" really is an expert in any meaningful sense. In other words, these folks are looking for approval.

Moving Beyond Approval

Within the business they've just started, of course, these entrepreneurs *are* the superior, but that simple fact isn't enough to undo years, perhaps decades, of workplace training. I've come in contact with "early entrepreneurs" who have lost countless hours of their own time and paid huge bills consulting with accountants, attorneys, and other business "experts" who supposedly "know how to proceed" in a given area.

Though your lawyers and accountants are important members of your team, they almost certainly don't know more than you do about your area of expertise, and they can't guarantee a positive outcome for you. With them or without them, you're likely to fall short a good percentage of the time. When that happens, you may be tempted to redouble your efforts to "gather all the data" before you move forward on the next decision. Are you really gathering data—or are you trying to find approval?

When something goes wrong, which will happen, a more rewarding approach is to put matters in perspective. Learn to recognize exactly what worked and what didn't, and in the process, you will learn to reinforce your own good business instincts. Try something. See what happens. Then step back and find out where your instincts paid off and where they didn't. Then get ready to try again. And if you're looking for a great way to gain market intelligence, establish contacts and share stories with other entrepreneurs. Forget about tracking down "experts." Attend a trade show that relates to your business or its customers—talk to people—and take as many notes as you possibly can. Then adjust your approach and—you guessed it—try again. That's how you become a real expert.

Don't shoot for perfection. Shoot for getting seventy-five percent of your business efforts working—and pointed at the right audience—seventy-five percent of the time. That's an excellent (and realistic) goal for someone who's launching a new business. If three-quarters of what you're shooting for works out three-quarters of the time—in terms of pricing, quality control, financial planning and management, person-to-person management, marketing, whatever—you'll be doing quite well.

Learn from administrative mistakes (try not to repeat them), but don't fixate on what went wrong, especially if you're dealing with areas where revenue is not seriously affected. Start-up businesses can fail (and have) because proprietors got so hung up on some administrative problem that they lost sight of critical sales and marketing issues, to cite a typical example. When "solving" a thorny, recurrent accounting problem deflects significant attention and time away from key prospects and customers, disaster looms—especially in one-person outfits.

There's nothing wrong with looking for advice or input on issues where you lack key information. That's what members of your network of personal contacts and public libraries are for. Likewise, there's nothing wrong with paying for information that is directly related to the (usually quite narrow) field of expertise of a qualified professional person. But if you're paying your attorney to discuss marketing ideas, or paying

your accountant to tell you what he thinks of your office layout, there's a problem. You're looking for approval from the
boss—and paying for that approval—when *you're* the boss.

There's an old saying in business: You can't inspect quality
into a product. If that's true—and I think it is—then it's
equally true that you can't *consult* good instincts into your
organization. You simply have to supply them yourself
through good old trial and error. In the vast majority of situations you will face as you launch and grow your business,
you will have to follow your own instincts. Sometimes your
instincts will be on target, sometimes they won't. But you can
count on two things:

- Small-business success is not the same as avoiding all
  error!
- Small-business failure is not the same as making a bad
  decision you learn something from.

These are hard lessons for some budding entrepreneurs to
grasp. People who get fixated on absolute accuracy, on *never*
making a mistake, on delivering *complete* information in any
and all situations, and on researching *everything* tend to have
a hard time when they try to start businesses. The truth is, no
entrepreneur gets it a hundred percent right all the time. And
there are times when risking a mistake in a particular area of
your business is a very good bet indeed.

Don't get me wrong. There's a place for perfectionism; it's
good (and even essential) in small doses. If your research indicates that customers expect a thirty percent input-output
ratio from your widgets, and you're stuck at twenty-five percent despite designs that indicate your product should be performing better, it's in your best interest to locate the problem
and not to stop until you do. But you simply can't expect to
get everything right on all fronts, all the time. A great many
transferees from the corporate world, used to marching in
place until a higher-up says something is "right," think otherwise. One way or another, they learn that the world of business is a world of informed guesses and revised approaches,

not cut-and-dried solutions. The same, I think, can be said of the world of politics and any number of other areas of human endeavor that must come to terms with the unknown.

Remember the seventy-five percent rule—and remember that great leaders are often great learners, improvisers, and risk-takers. Most of our most celebrated entrepreneurs, politicians, and inventors accepted and even embraced the risks associated with leadership.

Follow their lead. Make informed decisions—but make decisions knowing that you may fall short and then learn something from the results you achieve. Franklin Delano Roosevelt said, "It is common sense to take a method and try it. If it fails, admit it frankly and try another—but above all, try something." There are worse words to live by as you try to deliver on the goals you set for your business and yourself.

7

THE PROS AND CONS OF STARTING FROM SCRATCH

When you start up a business, you need to have more than just a great idea and a vision. You also need to know how you are going to approach your business—that is, of the many organizational structures you can choose from, you need to decide which will provide the best foundation for marketing and selling your idea. You may also want to examine the option of buying a franchise or a preexisting business, rather than starting a company from scratch. This chapter examines some of the options you have to consider, and includes one unique suggestion about a way to launch a start-up with a little help from some friends.

Legalities

The legal structure of your business has a direct effect on many aspects of your operations, chief among them being what your tax liability is going to be and how potential investors will view you. If you are starting your business from scratch, then you will have to decide whether your business is going to be a sole proprietorship, a partnership, or a corporation. There are advantages and disadvantages to each of these options, so you may find it beneficial to consult with an attorney or accountant who can advise you as to what will work best for your purposes.

The simplest and most popular business structure is the *sole proprietorship,* in which there is one sole owner of a business (this may also be a husband-and-wife team, which would be considered one owner). Most of the advice in this book, in fact, proceeds on the assumption that you are a sole proprietor, someone who has started a business from scratch and is assuming all the profits and all the losses.

If you enter into a *partnership,* then you co-own the business with one or more other persons, who share in the profits and losses—and the workload. An ideal partnership often involves three people who each bring separate sets of skills and expertise into the business. Each will also contribute an amount of money to the start-up funds and have a financial stake in the firm.

Finally, a *corporation* is a business owned by a group of people—the shareholders. Many people opt for incorporation because it allows better protection of one's personal assets in the event of legal problems than a partnership or a sole proprietorship. In a small business, you will most likely have anywhere from five to thirty-five shareholders, who have a say in how the business is run because of the money they have invested in your company. This investment gives them voting power to elect the company's chief executive and other operating officers. The amount of power they wield depends on the amount of money they have invested (for which they receive dividends). In general, corporations are more successful at raising capital than proprietorships or partnerships. If you are thinking of incorporation, you need to consider what effect that will have on your tax liability and personal finances. As attractive as incorporation may seem to you, there are a lot of hidden dangers you need to learn about—chief among them the possibility that you'll be taxed twice for the same money.

Which you choose will depend, of course, on the number of owners involved in the business and the amount of money they have invested in your company. Bear in mind that the more people who are involved, the more complex your business becomes in just about every aspect. So get plenty of advice before making the jump into incorporation, and carefully weigh the pros and cons of your other two options. You should also ask your attorney about the possibility of setting up an S corporation, which can carry important tax advantages on the federal level. Chances are good, though, that for your start-up purposes, a sole proprietorship or a partnership would be the best way to go.

Manufacturing and Service Businesses

When you start a business, you have to decide whether it's going to be manufacturing-oriented, service-oriented, or a combination of the two.

A manufacturing start-up has a definite physical item (such as bicycle helmets or children's toys) that must be produced, marketed, and shipped to a specified market. You have to consider all the logistics of how and where the products are going to be produced, what it's going to cost you to manufacture them, the number of workers you'll need to keep production up, salaries, liability insurance, and so on. This is true even if you are currently doing everything right in your own home. If your business takes off—as you no doubt hope it will—then your home will soon be unable to accommodate your operation, and you'll have to explore other alternatives for your business's physical location.

A service start-up is based on a particular service or solution (such as cleaning antique cars or performing annual income tax–preparation services) that you can offer to specific customers. Because you don't have manufacturing costs to consider, a service start-up may be a lot less expensive to get off the ground. However, if it involves training team members—both in the technical demands of their work and in the customer-first orientation that makes success possible—it is often quite a challenge.

Whether yours is a manufacturing or a service start-up or a combination of the two, there is another thing to consider—office space and resources. One unique option you may want to explore, depending on your financial situation and how you feel about the potentially lonely prospect of working on your own, is a business incubator. This method can provide an ideal way to get your feet in the water without getting so wet that you have a hard time getting out. Furthermore, it is a highly cost-efficient way of getting a business started.

Simply put, a business incubator is like a mother hen. Your company is placed with other start-up companies to share office space and equipment, including the cost of rentals, leases, utilities, administrative support, and so on. By sharing the expenses with others in the same situation, you can save money and invest it in those areas of your business that will get it up and running faster. You can also benefit from the services provided at reduced rates or even pro bono by the mother incubator—for instance, lawyers, sales representatives, accountants, and consultants.

Business incubators are largely funded by nonprofit and government organizations, but may also be affiliated with universities. There are currently more than five hundred business incubators throughout the nation. If this is an option that interests you, you can find out more by calling the National Business Incubation Association (located in Athens, Ohio) at 614–593–4331. I recommend, however, that you investigate this option thoroughly before trying it—and that includes talking to people who have done it.

Starting from scratch, however, may not be the best thing for you, no matter how it's done. There's a lot of time and effort and paperwork involved in getting a business off the ground that many budding entrepreneurs would like to just skip over. In addition, you may be one of those people who wants to go into business for himself or herself but doesn't have a fabulous idea on which to build a company. For that matter, you may simply feel you haven't enough business experience to launch something from scratch. In this case, you are probably considering buying a franchise or an already established business that you can start running immediately, without the fuss and bother—and risks—of getting an idea launched and established in the marketplace.

Simply put, a franchise is a legal arrangement that exists between the parent organization, known as the franchisor, and the business owner, who is the franchisee. The franchisee pays for the rights to use the franchisor's name and sell its products according to set guidelines and requirements. Fast-food establishments such as McDonald's and Wendy's are among the best-known franchising opportunities, but franchises exist in just about all sectors of the economy.

The great advantage of buying a franchise is that you can run it easily by following the procedures provided to you and by taking advantage of the resources and expert help available from the parent organization. The support of the franchisor also makes it easier for a franchisee to obtain financing from lending institutions. The downside of franchising is that you will generally be restricted to running your business according to the franchisor's strict requirements. You will be told what you can sell, what you can charge, what you can or cannot do in the way of decor, how you can advertise, and even how your employees should dress. You have to be prepared to accept these restrictions if you decide to purchase a franchise. If you're more of a freethinker who likes to do things his or her own way, then this option probably isn't for you.

If you decide to buy a franchise, make sure that you do your homework well and pick one that suits your particular interests and skills. Check out the various industries and what they have to offer. Franchising opportunities are posted on the Internet and listed in your local newspapers. When you've identified a possible opportunity, spend some time checking it out to make sure that it's a viable option for you. How much up-front investment is required? What kinds of people have turned the franchise into a success? How does the franchise stack up in annual ratings published in major magazines? What kind of marketing support will be available to you?

Research the opportunity well and ask questions that will help you to determine whether it fits into your objective. Spend some time visiting a franchise location and talking to the owner and the employees. If you make the decision to buy, I strongly recommend that you get some professional help when it comes to handling negotiations, contracts, and other issues.

If the marketing, operational, and business-development restrictions posed by franchising are not for you (and those restrictions can be significant), then you may want to consider buying a preexisting business. The best bet is one that has been up and running for some time and either has proven successful or has the potential for growth—and preferably both.

Buying a business has all the advantages that we have previously discussed, but it's not without its risks. You have to be extremely careful about examining every aspect of a business before you make the decision to buy. This includes analyzing its financial statements and tax returns for the last three to five years to ensure that it is in sound condition and has viable sales and operating expenses within the industry standard. In other words, you have to determine what the business is really worth. You will need the help of an accountant or a tax attorney with this. Other areas to examine include the company's payables and receivables, its employees, its customers, its competitors, its location and physical appearance, its physical assets such as inventory and equipment, and what sort of public image the company maintains.

Finally, you need to ensure that all its legal paperwork is in order and can be easily transferred to you.

Once you have identified the business you want to buy, you have to come to an agreement with the current owner on how the transaction will take place. You may want to acquire it gradually, over a period of time; lease it from the owner with the option to buy at a later date; establish a marketing agreement that gives you the right to market a particular product within a specified area (similar to a franchise, but with fewer restrictions); or have a management contract in which you manage the business for a fee and retain the option to buy if things work to your satisfaction. All of these options have the advantage of enabling you to back out of the deal if it doesn't work out for you, something that an outright purchase doesn't give you.

You may decide that the opportunity is superb and opt for outright purchase as the simplest, most acceptable choice for your purposes. Bear in mind, though, that you are taking a bigger risk by going the full-purchase route, particularly if there are setbacks or losses in the future. By keeping the current owner involved to any extent, you are giving yourself a safety net in case of any unforeseen problems.

There is a great deal of research and legwork you have to do to find the business you want to buy, and you may want to spare yourself all that time and effort. If this is the case, consider utilizing the services of a business broker. This is someone who functions in much the same way as a real estate agent. A broker will match the needs of a buyer with those of a seller and handle most of the arrangements between the two parties. When using a broker, take care to find the one who is best suited to meet your needs. Interview potential brokers to determine how much experience they have in the type of business you're looking into. Find out what their success rate is. Ask for references. Make sure the broker understands exactly what you're looking for and what your financial requirements are. A good broker will make sure that you, in turn, really know what you want and how much money you have to do it with. He or she should provide a business profile of every firm being offered for your consideration. Most important, there should be proof that he or she considers you a serious buyer and works diligently in your interests.

You may be tempted to sign up with a brokerage firm rather than with an individual broker. The danger in this is that the larger firms may be more interested in larger deals and cover a broader spectrum of deals, which may keep you from receiving the individualized attention you want. You're probably better off casting your lot with an individual or with a small firm that specializes in the area that interests you.

Understanding the pros and cons of the business option that you are pursuing and doing your homework well are crucial to making the decision that's right for you. Preparation is everything!

8

WHY YOU ARE ALWAYS YOUR OWN BEST SALESPERSON

One of the classic mistakes that nonsalespeople make in starting a business is to tell themselves that since they have never learned how to sell in any formal sense, they should hire a salesperson. They think that they should pay for someone who will handle all the details, contact all the customers, and close all the deals. I believe that in the vast majority of cases that's a big mistake.

Mind you, I'm not talking about partnership situations where one person handles the sales work and the other person takes on the design or manufacturing aspects of the business. That's a perfectly workable arrangement, one many, many entrepreneurs have succeeded with. The mistake lies in assuming that someone from outside the dynamic, creative center of your business will be as motivated, as knowledgeable, as energetic, or as persuasive about selling your product as you.

Skittishness about broadening their personal horizons

keeps many entrepreneurs from taking advantage of the person with the best sales potential in their organization—themselves. Instead, they hire outsiders, thinking that will help them become more effective. The reality is, you are almost certainly the best person to sell your product or service—you're in a position to do that better than anybody else. After all, you started your business. Who knows the product or service better than you? If you do not use your own expertise to sell your business, then there is a very good chance that your undertaking will not be successful. Consider the following questions:

- Who's more likely to respond creatively, responsibly, and accurately to a pressing problem raised by a key customer? ☐ You. ☐ A salesperson you hire from the outside.
- Who's more likely to ignore or conceal critical feedback—positive or negative—learned from your customer base? ☐ You. ☐ A salesperson you hire from the outside.
- Who's more likely to pass along confidential information to a competitor, say, a year from now? ☐ You. ☐ A salesperson you hire from the outside.
- Who's more likely to put in extra time, effort, or energy to keep existing customers happy? ☐ You. ☐ A salesperson you hire from the outside.
- Who's more likely to mislead a prospect or customer—or make a wildly inaccurate estimate—about turnaround time or performance? ☐ You. ☐ A salesperson you hire from the outside.
- Who's likely to have the most credibility with your customers and prospects? ☐ You. ☐ A salesperson you hire from the outside.

You get the picture. I'm not suggesting that there will *never* be a time in your company's development when hiring an outside salesperson (or a fleet of them!) will make all the sense in the world. But I am saying that during the crucial first year or so of your company's existence—when new revenue means everything to your operation, when relationships with customers and prospective customers are just beginning to blossom, when cash is tight—there's very little room for error. Mistakes that you can resolve without much incident in the third or fourth year can shut you down for good in the first year.

A large percentage of first-time entrepreneurs fool themselves about why they are hiring a salesperson. They tell themselves it's because they are unqualified to act in a sales capacity. In fact, it's because they don't know whether they're qualified to act in a sales capacity—and they don't really want to find out.

You will always represent yourself better than anyone else, for a number of reasons. For one thing, you're supremely motivated; for another, you've usually got all the information there is to have about your product or service. You understand your own business better than anyone else does, and what's more, you understand why you went into business in the first place. You treat this undertaking seriously. This is not a stopgap job or a way to fill up some part-time hours. It's something that you really want to do.

Consider, too, that a salesperson costs money—and that you won't always know which one is going to work out and which one won't. When I make this point to new entrepreneurs, they often offer a solution that seems, from a certain angle, to solve the problem: "I'll hire someone on full commission." There are flaws in this answer, though. First, you're probably not going to get anybody working on full commission who's really serious about the work—or at least no one nearly as serious about it as you are. Second, if you pay a big commission, which is probably what you'll have to do, that will deplete the income that you'll be making—and that's a trade-off you will want to think long and hard about making in the early stages. (If cash is very tight, of course, you may have no choice if you are determined to hire an outsider.) But whether you're paying full commission or establishing some other kind of compensation structure, the person you select has to be trained and has to be monitored, and that eats into your time.

You're actually far better off hiring someone to do, for instance, the production or the design, or else doing it yourself later during the day, than you are hiring a salesperson. Perhaps, like many, you'll say to yourself, "But I'm the president of the company. How does the president of a company make sales calls?" Expertly, that's how! I've been doing precisely that for seventeen years—calling prospects on the phone and going on sales calls—and I'm here to tell you that no one else in a given organization has the visibility, the knowledge, the authority, or the ability to get through to key decision makers that the president of the outfit does. When the receptionist—or anyone else—hears, "John Smith, President of ABC Company," you're more likely to get through, and you're more likely to be taken seriously by the people you reach. I know one entrepreneur who's managed to handle all the sales work for his company *and* put in some effective hours on the product-development front at the end of the day. But the sales work comes first! He's put his personal reputation, his prestige as head of the company to work—developing revenue sources. In the vast majority of cases, that's what first-time entrepreneurs should be doing.

Will learning to take on the sales role be a stretch for you? If you've never done any kind of selling before, it probably will. But wasn't stretching yourself a little, taking on new challenges, part of the reason you decided to start your own business in the first place? Most of the entrepreneurs I talk to say *yes* when I ask them that question, and I'm willing to bet that, deep down, you feel the same way about it.

I feel so strongly about the importance of not relying on outside sales help in your business's early years that I've devoted a large chunk of this book to helping nonsalespeople master the art of selling for themselves. In Part III you'll find, among other things, a wealth of simple, easy-to-implement strategies you can use to get yourself up to speed in this area. I can't promise that you'll never be intimidated by the process

of learning to interact with customers and prospective customers—sales can be a demanding line of work—but I can
promise that learning how to handle the sales function at the
top level of your new company will save you time, money,
and administrative hassles during an absolutely critical period. I can also promise you that, by committing to be your
own salesperson, you'll be in a position to develop much,
much stronger initial relationships with customers than you
would if you delegated the task to someone else.

At the beginning, then, the message is simple: Use your
precious cash for something else besides hiring an outside
salesperson. Start small, start direct, and start strong. If your
business requires personal selling, nominate yourself to do it
during the first year of operation, at least. You'll get all the
details on how to pull off that difficult job later on in this
book.

Don't let fear of the unknown keep you from taking advantage of the best salesperson you've got—you.

9

HANDLING FAMILY ISSUES

Many small-business owners become so consumed with starting and running their business that they neglect one of the most important aspects of their decision: how it will affect the people they love. Don't let this happen to you—especially if yours is a family-run business.

Because our work can often affect our attitudes and our attitudes more often than not affect our families, it follows that our families are almost always affected by our work. If you have a bad day at the office, you might come home grumpy and uncommunicative. If you were angry at somebody but didn't express your anger, you might very well snap at your spouse that evening. If you get tied up in meetings or on a prolonged phone conversation, you could very well forget that you were supposed to go to your son's violin recital at four.

You undoubtedly had experiences like these even when you were working for somebody else. More time spent on work obligations means less time spent on family, and on occasion, this can strain your personal relationships. That strain can become pretty severe, however, when it's your own business. The hours you have to put in may be double those involved in working for somebody else, and finding time for your family becomes that much more difficult. It's not good for them, and it's not good for you. For their part, they may feel neglected and resentful that they're not getting enough of your attention. It may seem to them that you care more about the business than you do about them. They will lose touch with you as you lose touch with them, and that can cause a lot of emotional pain. For your part, you may feel more removed from their lives than you want to be.

This picture is on the extreme side, but it describes what could happen if you neglect your family for the sake of your business. You may be especially fortunate and have loved ones who totally understand and support you in all you do. But it is still important for you to think of them as you go about launching and running your business—for your sake as much as for theirs. If your business is turning you into a workaholic, in fact, it may be time to stop and examine your priorities. Your business is the primary means by which you support your family—but what good does that do you if you have no real connection with them aside from the financial one? If you don't take time to relax and enjoy the people you love, if you're not really involved in their lives, nor they in yours, then you might as well be living with strangers.

So carve a special niche for family in your schedule, and stick to that schedule when you do. Make the time that you spend with them quality time, with no business interruptions. Keep the promises you make to your offspring to attend their school events and to take them to the circus or the ball game. Go out on a date with your spouse and plan the occasional romantic evening. Listen and interact, and get to know what is going on in the lives of those you love. The more you do to keep your relationships with family members healthy and balanced, the better it will be for both you and them.

It could be that you started your business because you thought it would allow you more time with your family. In fact, the opposite may often be true, unless you are working out of your own home. Even then, there will be problems to cope with, chief among them a frequent lack of quiet and privacy, not to mention the interruptions that will break your concentration on your work.

Personal problems can become magnified if yours is a family-owned or family-operated business. Granted, there are numerous advantages to employing members of your family in your business, chief among them the financial aspects. Many small-business owners start out by using family exclusively because they can skimp on salary and benefits and have an easier time with taxes and other forms. In addition, if the children employed are still minors, their parents don't have to pay the Social Security tax. Perhaps the biggest advantage of all in employing members of your family is that they will most likely share your commitment and dedication to the company. When everybody has a vested interest in the success of the company, there is more teamwork and more striving together for shared goals. And there is also the aspect of leadership succession. A family-owned business almost guarantees that somebody will be there to take over the company someday and keep the tradition going. All in all, a family-centered business can be a really great way to start.

But this arrangement has its downside, too. Just because people are part of your family doesn't mean they're going to agree with you all the time. If a consensus is not reached on what the company goals are, how they are going to be attained, and the role that each family member is to play, there is a possibility for discord that may tear apart the fabric not only of your business but also of your family! Clear lines have to be drawn regarding who has responsibility for what and who is the final decision maker when all else fails. Systems need to be developed so that all family members feel they are an important part of the operation, no matter what their position in it. If there's any chance at all that rivalries and feuds might disrupt the smooth running of your company as well as familial harmony, then you're better off finding alternatives to involving relatives in the business.

"It'll never happen in my family," you say? Don't be so sure. You'll be faced with such issues as what to do if your son starts slacking off, or how to respond when your spouse makes an important decision without consulting you. Even when you make it clear that you're in charge, hidden resentments that you might not encounter from a nonfamily member could potentially undermine your authority and affect your relationship on a personal level. The fact is, there will be problems and issues to deal with that are not part of the everyday running-a-business norm. Too many families start out certain that they can work together harmoniously, without disagreement. But even those who share the same genes can look at things very differently and become stubborn and argumentative about their point of view. It's human nature.

So be prepared for what you are letting yourself in for when you hire family members. Make sure they thoroughly understand their role in the company, what is expected of them, and who's in charge of what.

Don't be afraid of making legal agreements with family members. This is especially true when it's not just a matter of hiring but of being in partnership with a spouse or relative. When you co-own a business with a family member, areas of responsibility should be clearly defined so as to leave no room for misunderstandings about who does what and where certain authority lies. A contractual agreement is certainly not out of the ordinary and should be drawn up before you go into business together. This is especially true if your business partner is your spouse. Many a harmonious marriage has broken up because of spousal disagreements over how the business should be run!

BRANCHING OUT

One of the important things I learned during my first few years in business for myself was that every day offered me the opportunity to become closer to my customers and potential customers—to learn more about them. Every sales call, whether it resulted in immediate revenue or not, was worthwhile in terms of the information I gained from the experience.

With every new undertaking, I was able to get a little better fix on the key questions that were driving my business. Who were my most likely customers? What issues were important to them? What goals were driving them, both in the short and the long terms? How realistic were my goals for a particular prospective customer, or for a whole group of customers? Which of those goals needed to be revised? A great many of my early "no sale" meetings turned into incredibly positive business experiences—because they pointed me toward new ways of structuring my business and helped me develop new services that people could use to improve what they were already doing.

In this section, you'll learn how you, too, can be more specific about what you offer and its benefits to others. The more specific you are about how what you provide helps out other people, the better off you're going to be.

10

YOUR MOST IMPORTANT ASSET:
WHAT YOU FOCUS ON

In the second part of this book we'll be looking at a lot of principles you can use as you formalize your business's "battle plan." None of those principles, however, will be as important as the one we'll be examining in this chapter: Your thoughts create your future.

When I talk about the importance of using your thoughts to build your business, I speak from personal experience. In my view, there's no such thing as luck, good or bad. There's no such thing as "getting the breaks." There's no such thing as "good days" or "bad days." There's only the way you think about what you're doing at the moment. Your attitude and the way you think about the present situation and the future direction of your company will have a direct impact on its success or failure. Not a *potential* impact . . . but a direct impact.

Before you can take full advantage of any of the other ideas that appear in this book, you must accept that it is you and you alone who control the outcome of your plans and actions, and that your mental attitude plays a direct and very meaningful role in how things happen.

The first and most powerful ingredient in your internal recipe for material success is to *expect success*—that is, you have to consider it inevitable and act accordingly. In practical terms, that means confronting seemingly impossible problems and sudden setbacks in a special way. You must do so without panicking, without focusing on the worst possible outcome, and without assuming that all is lost. To the contrary, you must be willing to find something in each new situation to be grateful for or at least to learn from, you must become adept at envisioning the best possible outcome, and you must, when face to face with a particularly trying challenge, adopt the attitude that "this too shall pass."

This is the confidence factor. You can't simply *hope* that all will work out; you must *act under the assumption* that your worthy aims are being fulfilled—and are even supported by The Powers That Be, however you define them.

It all starts with a vision. When you first conceived your business idea, you probably visualized exactly how your product or service would be used and the benefits that would accrue to those who used it. That's a start. But a true visionary also anticipates the impact his or her idea will have on the market and the rewards that will come with success. There is nothing wrong with envisioning yourself enjoying the payoff from implementing your great idea. So do so! Find a way to turn your goal into something tangible, something you can focus on right now and throughout your day. That might take the form of a photograph of a beloved family member—the person you're doing all this for—or a specific material reward you're working toward—that Cadillac you'll buy when you've hit your first- or second-year income goal. Whatever you do, find an image that will help you hold on to your initial vision! Find one that will help to sustain you through the most challenging days and nights, one that will provide fuel to the internal fire that keeps you going as you pursue your dream.

If you truly believe it will happen—if you expect it to happen, if you act as though it is happening, if you commit yourself to doing everything necessary to make it happen—then it will happen! Your expectation will give you the courage to take the steps necessary to turn your vision into tangible success.

To achieve that kind of commitment to your vision, you must evaluate what does and doesn't support the achievement of your goals. I recommend that you sit down with a pen and a piece of paper and make three columns. In the first column, list the qualities you possess that can be considered weaknesses in your character or in your abilities (for instance, a tendency toward procrastination). In the second column, list your strongest qualities (for instance, a high personal energy level). In the third column, list the qualities you don't currently possess that are most needed to achieve what you want to accomplish (say, the ability to prioritize the items on your to-do list effectively). When this is done, take another piece of paper and write out a new vision for yourself. Be specific; imagine what you are going to look like and how you are going to feel when you attain your goals. Describe the things you will have and the actions you will take. In other words, describe the person you want to become, combining all your strongest qualities *and* those from the third column that you still need to develop. Your aim is to eliminate all the weaknesses in the first column. You don't want them to exist anymore; therefore you are going to exclude them from your written vision—and from your consciousness.

Another thing you want to eliminate is negative thoughts. This is not easy. But if negativity invades your thinking, then failure is sure to follow close behind. The power of positive thinking is one of the greatest powers of all. It can pull you out of the deepest holes and set you back on the right path. One sign that you are giving in to negative thinking is when you begin to experience doubts about your abilities or your decisions. Don't let self-doubt sabotage your efforts! First of all, self-doubt will make you appear weak and uncertain to others. Second, it will sap your energy and ability to function effectively. Take the time to make good decisions; then, once a decision has been made or an action has been taken, accept the consequences and avoid second-guessing yourself. You will rarely know with absolute certainty beforehand that something will work; you can only do your best to make it work. In reality, there is no such thing as a "correct" or an "incorrect" decision. There is only your decision, and you have to believe in that decision—just as you have to believe in yourself—and be ready to apply its results intelligently.

When times are tough, when every little thing seems to be getting you down, stop a minute, take a deep breath, and take a new look at the situation. Ask yourself, "What can I learn from this?" Chances are good that you'll see something you may have missed previously—an insight that lights the way to improvement, or an opportunity that you overlooked because you were consumed by the problem rather than searching for a solution. If nothing else, you will discover what you did wrong this time so that you won't do it again the next time. Conversely, you should reinforce your successes by understanding what you did right and making it a part of your map for the future. There is always a silver lining to any situation, because every situation is a learning experience.

Errors are nothing to be afraid of; we all make them, day in and day out! Some mistakes are minor and can be remedied in an instant; others require "major surgery" to repair the damage. Some mistakes we generate ourselves; others may be generated by an employee or a supplier. The question is, What can you learn from that mistake in order to prevent it from happening again? How can you prevent similar mistakes from happening? Take time to examine the cause of the error and look for an effective remedy. You want to deal with mistakes proactively, not reactively.

Once again, the attitude you take means everything to the outcome. If you mentally berate yourself for every error (for example, "How could I have been so stupid as to . . . ?") you will find it hard to learn from your mistakes. If, on the other hand, you say to yourself, "Well, it happened—so where do I go from here?" then you're making it possible for you to move forward in a positive direction.

Failure doesn't happen until you admit it as a possibility. You will, however, experience some powerful "temporary setbacks" to your goals! The key is to approach them properly. They are an inevitable part of building a business. You have to learn from them and move on. This is why tenacity is so crucial to your success. You have to do your best to overcome the feelings of fatigue or frustration by asking, "What can I learn from this?"

Take a Break!

Speaking of fatigue, here's an important piece of advice: Know when to relax. If this seems contrary to what I've stressed about long hours of hard work, it's not. Everybody needs time to stop and refuel. Exhaustion serves no purpose except to put unnecessary stress on you and potentially on your relationships with others. You have to have the ability to "let things go" at the end of the day, especially when circumstances become intense.

You also need to be able to take time out for yourself to do things you enjoy that are not work-related. All work and no play will only wear you out. So *make time for yourself:* Read a good book; take the kids to the park; go to a movie with your spouse; visit a museum with a friend; take up a hobby; try yoga or meditation. Do things that will take you away from the business, even if it's only for a few hours. Taking a break from work also plays a part in your refueling process. When you return to your work, you will find yourself more energized and focused.

This is true even during a full workday. For example, if your work requires you to spend long hours at the computer, then take frequent, short breaks to rest your eyes, stretch your legs, or give your weary mind a momentary respite. Ten-minute breaks every one to two hours or so will do wonders for you, both physically and mentally!

You may be fortunate enough to have a mentor or adviser who has offered to provide guidance as you start up your company, or perhaps you know another entrepreneur who has been successful on both a professional and personal level. These people are certain to have recipes of their own for staying on top of things mentally. Talk to them. Often, the simple act of sharing the challenges you face in your business will energize you and help you recommit to your goal.

To my way of thinking, a successful entrepreneur is somebody who knows how to take care of a young business's most important asset—the entrepreneur. This person has what I call selective tunnel vision about her goals: She knows when to step back and recharge the batteries—*and* when to get back in the game so she can create opportunities and find solutions that support her vision and her goals.

So learn to think big—even when you're starting out small. Practice putting an entrepreneurial positive spin on the next setback or downer you experience in your everyday life. Whether it's an interruption from a talkative telemarketer, a tough meeting, or a call you're not looking forward to making, stop for just a moment and ask yourself, "What can I learn from this? And does it really make sense to beat myself up over it when I could be focusing on something more positive and energizing?" Once you can learn to step back from that situation and retain your positive focus, you'll be well on your way to developing a skill you'll be using again and again as you build your business.

11

FINDING YOUR BUSINESS NICHE

A person walks down the street of a neighborhood with both apartments and small shops and notices that there's no dry cleaner within two or three miles. He thinks to himself, "That's a long way to have to walk or drive to drop off a suit. I'll bet a dry-cleaning operation could make money in this neighborhood." He opens up a shop, and it's a success. A year or so goes by, and one day, someone else walks by to drop off some dry cleaning; it's around noon, and this person thinks to herself, "Gee, there sure are a lot of professional people swinging by this dry-cleaning shop around lunchtime, and if they want to pick up something to eat, all they can do is swing into that convenience store. I'll bet a delicatessen would do well here." So she opens a delicatessen, and it's a success. Another year or so goes by, and one day, someone else notices that lots of professional people are visiting the dry cleaner and the delicatessen, but there's no small restaurant with table service in the area. Guess what happens?

That's how businesses are built; that's how cities and towns are built. A little bit at a time.

A city is made up of people who have found niches within the marketplace, often creating their businesses in between businesses that already exist. There are big businesses all around us—big boulders, I like to call them—and we don't need to compete with the big business. We need to find a place for ourselves. Even a small business can find a crack between the boulders and manage to keep a group of customers happy.

My firm, DEI, is a sales-training company; we work for large companies and train their salespeople to be more effective. We are not the largest player on the block, nor do we have to be. The sales-training business is a $20 billion business; even if I quadrupled my business overnight, it wouldn't come anywhere close to $20 billion! Nor does it need to. My business needs to support the people I employ and my family, and it needs to be saleable at some point. I can achieve those objectives without being the biggest sales-training company in the country. I found a situation that works well for me. I understand that not everybody is going to buy from me, nor do they have to. I just need my piece of the pie. You need to think that way, too.

Think about emerging marketplaces. For example, in the year 2020 it's projected there will be over 350 million people living in the United States. Think about what that means. Think about the number of pagers, telephones, televisions, lamps, lights, tables, refrigerators, homes, car tires, that all those people will need. Then figure out what's needed to support those businesses. Don't concentrate on going into the big businesses, because that's probably not going to happen. Concentrate on the small businesses.

You may have heard the story of Stanley H. Kaplan. You may not know him by name, but you probably do know his operation, which is called Kaplan Educational Centers. It's one of the largest providers of SAT training in the United States. In 1960 Stanley Kaplan realized that there were hundreds of high school students in the New York City area who were not getting into college because they did not score high enough on the SATs. He had found a niche in the market. His training centers grew over time and now the business is owned by a major corporation. He retired a rich and happy man. But it all started with a clearly defined business niche.

How many businesses are there like Kaplan's? Thousands upon thousands. You need only find a place where you can create your foothold, your ledge that you can pull yourself onto. You need to see your vision and understand it. For example, right now we're seeing that copiers are becoming more important and more sophisticated, the World Wide Web and the Internet are growing, and television cable stations need product, all of which means that more people are entering into those marketplaces. We have tremendous opportunities today to find places to work where we've never worked before, but you have to be creative in thinking about this.

The other day I was driving in Florida and I was behind a truck that had a bumper sticker with a telephone number and message on it. It said, "How am I doing? Call us at 1–800 . . ." I looked at the number and wrote it down. Later I called the company up. The company provides a third party to check on the company's vehicles. In other words, if you don't like the way they're being driven, you call the third-party company and they report the driver to the company that employs that person. Here's somebody who created a business out of that. And my firm got business from them by helping them sell to other companies!

The massive size of our economy means that there are always going to be new opportunities, new niches. You only have to find one that works for you. You have to find someone who will benefit from what you do—someone to whom you can say, "Hey, are you looking for a way to encourage your drivers to drive safely? You can lower your insurance costs if you work with us. Put this bumper sticker on the back of each truck—most of your drivers will start driving more responsibly, and the few who don't will be reported to you automatically!"

How many trucking companies could benefit from that program? Thousands! When a definable group of people can benefit from what you do—whether you're opening a dry-cleaning store or helping trucking companies pay less in insurance premiums—that's a niche. Find yours!

12

THINKING YOUR WAY THROUGH THE FIRST YEAR—AND BEYOND

Let's say you and your family have lived in an apartment for six years, and you've decided that you want to build a house. You tell your husband or wife that you're planning to move in six months, and you start to make all the arrangements. You buy your lot. You arrange for someone to take over your apartment. You start buying furniture for the new place.

Then you talk to an architect. You tell him about the style you want and the amount of money you're prepared to pay for the house. He's enthusiastic about the project and agrees to take it on. But when you ask him how long he thinks the whole project will take—from beginning to end—he says, "At least a year," and your heart sinks. You argue back and forth for a while, but the best commitment you can get out of him is one year. There are going to be some compromises. You should have talked with the architect first.

Thinking Realistically About the First Year

Most people have a similar problem when they start planning what their first year or so in business will look like. They think it will take them less time to get "up and running" than it really will.

What do I mean by "up and running"? Well, I don't mean what a lot of people *think* I mean. I'm not talking about simply attracting clients or customers during your first year. The truth is that even though there may be some challenges when it comes to securing financing, traditional or otherwise, a great many first-time entrepreneurs begin their experiment in self-employment with commitments for some kind of revenue from their existing contact base. (Most of us would be understandably hesitant to leave a current job if we had no prospects whatsoever for our new business.) But winning a first assignment or getting a first order is really not all that difficult, especially if you're using goodwill you've developed in previous professional settings. What's really tough is winning *repeat* business . . . and developing customers who not only think highly of what you do but are willing to ask you to do it again, and perhaps even step up and recommend you to other people.

One of the most common mistakes first-time entrepreneurs make in their first year is failing to ask themselves, "What do I have to do today to ensure that the business is moving closer to delivering on the goals that I've set for six months, a year, two years, or longer from now?" In most cases, the best answer to that question will have something to do with prospecting for new business *beyond your limited, existing base of contacts.*

The cash challenges you face during the first year may be dramatic, but they shouldn't stop you from finding new people to whom you can deliver top-notch products or services. If you focus only on your current contacts, you're very likely to launch what I call a "boomerang start-up"—that is, a temporary leave of absence from the world of the employed. People who launch "boomerang start-ups" work for a company; then they work for themselves for a year or so; then they go back to working for a company again.

Even if you're totally financed, even if you have all the money you think you will need, you almost certainly will still need to develop a *new* prospect base to get your business up and running. You'll need to work with new people and you'll need to work out the kinks in what you have to offer, in order to make that repeat-customer scenario a reality.

Many of the entrepreneurs I've spoken with have enough financing and/or first-time customers to make surviving the first year of business a realistic possibility. But what will their position be then? All too often, the pattern is an unhealthy one: This ability to "tread water" on their own during the first year leads to a decision to expand heedlessly and overcommit in the second year, which leads to major organizational crises in the third year. The goal is not simply to survive the first year, but to build a company—that is, develop something you could conceivably sell to another person at some point. It's not just enduring the freshman year of business that counts; it's laying the foundation for success in the sophomore, junior, and senior years of business.

The longer you put off the job of reaching out to brand-new business prospects, the longer you wait to get feedback from customers who aren't afraid of hurting your feelings or damaging a friendship, the greater the disservice you'll be doing to your business. Eventually, you'll find that even "inside accounts" don't pan out.

What's going to happen is that the people on the other side of the table—that is, the person you're selling to, the person you're buying from, the people who are lending you money or not lending you money—aren't going to play by your rules. They're going to play by their rules. And especially if you have borrowed money from friends, relatives, banks, or other sources, you're going to be in for a rude awakening. Once your business doesn't perform at the level you thought it would—once you realize that house isn't going to be completed for at least a year—you're going to wish you had something in process.

So my advice for the first year is to think ahead. Don't wait until the bottom falls out and then realize how important it is to sell.

You need to have a long-term plan and a daily plan of discipline in order to be successful, and they have to be linked to the buying cycle of the industry in which you're operating. Let's now take a look at some of the numbers you're likely to be up against.

Don't Waste the First Three Months

The first three months of business are precious, so use them wisely. Take the time to set up your business: You'll be making sales calls. You'll be making appointments. You'll be talking to people about what you do. You may or may not bring in some existing business. But if you do have existing projects, *don't* make the mistake of working exclusively on them and neglecting or postponing your new marketing efforts.

One classic mistake beginning entrepreneurs make is what I call the getting-the-brochure-printed syndrome. I have nothing against brochures—but I have a problem with brochures that cause all other marketing work to be neglected during that critical first three-month period when a business is launched. Small-business owners tell themselves they have to get brochures printed. Those brochures have to be written, which takes anywhere from one to two weeks; they've got to be edited, so that's another two weeks; perhaps they've got to be corrected before they go to press—that's another two weeks. Add everything up, including the printing time, and it's easily a month and a half or two months before they're done. In the meantime, the business owner deludes himself into thinking that something is happening on the marketing front because someone's working on brochures somewhere.

In other words, what the average small-business owner says is, "I'll wait until I get my brochures before I really announce myself." That's a big mistake. You can start announcing yourself immediately. You don't need a lot to go into business. You just need yourself, a telephone, and a desk. (Part III of this book will guide you through setting up your person-to-person promotional and marketing plan.)

Don't Assume You'll Get Paid Soon

Another classic mistake is being overly optimistic when setting up cash-flow plans for your business—assuming that business will materialize quickly (it won't) or that your customers will pay their bills promptly (they won't, and companies don't have any hesitation about asking small businesses like yours to be patient when it comes to settling up).

Let's assume it will take you three months to generate a new customer. That means that every single day that you do not make an appointment, or every day that you do not initiate a new contact will add an additional day to that three-month period. In other words, if you start two days after day one, then you will not see a sale for two days after month three, which means you're prolonging the time until you get paid. And, as I say, that's not automatic, either!

Let's assume you're a consultant working with companies in a particular industry; you win a commitment, and you go ahead and do your assignment. It takes you anywhere from three to six months to complete that assignment. You then bill your client. In theory you're going to get paid right away, but in reality, you're not—no matter who you're working with. The company is going to delay payment for anywhere from ten days to ten months, depending upon the size of the company. That's right—ten months! So if the assignment takes you three months to secure, and three months to complete, and you don't get paid for another, say, three months after that, that's at least nine months until you receive income!

These are the kinds of figures you'll need to enter into your cash-flow estimates. If you've already made estimates about how much money is likely to be coming into your new firm, this would be a good opportunity to review them and ask yourself how realistic they are. How far deep in "the hole" are you likely to go?

The completed cash-flow worksheet illustrated here is one you may be able to use as a model for your own work on paper or a computer spreadsheet program.

Can you make the outlook a little less dire? Perhaps. You may be able to negotiate prepayment arrangements—where you're paid a certain percentage up front, before the project moves forward—or negotiate to be paid as the project moves along. But, nevertheless, the larger companies will not pay you the day that you think you're going to get paid. They'll delay that payment.

Take the opportunity now to develop a cash-flow estimate

EXHIBIT 3

Condensed Cash-Flow Worksheet (6 months)

	JAN	FEB	MAR	APR	MAY	JUNE
TOTAL EST. INFLOW						
TOTAL EST. OUTFLOW						
CASH AVAILABLE						

EXHIBIT 4

Sample Condensed Cash-Flow Worksheet (6 months)
(assumes monthly expenses of $3,000, first sale on January 1, first payment by end of March)

	JAN	FEB	MAR	APR	MAY	JUNE
TOTAL EST. INFLOW	—	—	1,500	3,000	3,000	4,000
TOTAL EST. OUTFLOW	3,000	3,000	3,000	3,000	3,000	3,000
CASH AVAILABLE	−3,000	−6,000	−7,500	−7,500	−7,500	−6,500

Financing required to meet lowest cash position: $7,500

that's *pessimistic* rather than *optimistic*. Determine what your lowest likely financial point is—and then you'll be better informed when it comes to securing the financing you need, which will be discussed in Chapter 17.

You also have to understand how you're going to finance the cash flow that's necessary to pay your existing bills, that is, your private bills—for your home, and so on—as well as the financial obligations of your business. You need to look at all that carefully and project out when you can expect to get payment. And, depending on the type of business you're running, you may have to build in some percentage of default payments, for those accounts that default on payments, despite your best efforts to collect.

The first year of business is perhaps the most difficult. And yet it is the most crucial because you set the groundwork for your second year, which will be successful if you worked during the first year. However, if you spent three months of the first year waiting for the brochures to get back from the printer, you cannot say you started then. You have to eliminate that first quarter in your thinking and realize that you actually started business three months later! That's an expensive proposition.

A word of caution is in order about clients and customers who "support" your efforts to start a business, those people you've built up a relationship with over the years who want to see you succeed and promise to give you some business to help you get started. The danger with these clients is that they often turn out to be only one-time clients. Often they'll give you all the business they think you can handle, which may be minimal, but you probably shouldn't count on them to turn into repeat customers. Some of these "clients" are interested simply in helping you get started, but not interested enough to make a formal long-term commitment to you. Don't bank on them.

Remember, every small business relies on some form of selling. You cannot get by without it. If you spend your first year burning up cash and setting up commitments and relationships that pay off big in the second year, then the first year is a success, not a failure, even if you only break even at the end of the fiscal year. If you ease off during the second year, focus on existing customers and new initiatives, and neglect to prospect for new business, then you're probably riding for a fall in year three—even if the numbers look good at the end of year two.

All of this advice is based on the presumption that you're trying to build equity within your business—trying to build an enterprise someone else might be interested in buying someday. There are plenty of examples of people who don't much care about building up their businesses in this way, but to me they're glorified freelancers, not entrepreneurs. To build a business, you need customers. And to get a fix on *how many* customers you'll need to meet challenges, you have to know what your income picture's going to look like three, six, or twelve months down the line. If you prepare properly in the beginning, you'll be more likely to have a successful outcome.

13

ESTABLISHING YOUR GOALS: THE ART OF THINKING BIG

The foundation for the business you build will be the goals that you set for it and for yourself. The right goals provide a sense of direction, a focus that is crucial to any entrepreneur (as well as to anyone *working with* an entrepreneur). They also provide the means by which you measure your progress, as well as the inspiration to continue; for as you achieve each goal, you are given the impetus to go on and strive for the next one.

Goals are most meaningful when they're tangible; you should write them down. (This point will be reviewed in detail in Chapter 15.) Many people, though, seem to fear setting goals for themselves. They don't want to commit to anything lest they fail, so they commit nothing to paper. They assume that as long as they have a general idea of what they're trying to accomplish, they don't need to write anything down.

This is a huge mistake. Writing out goals is an important step toward attaining them. And you aren't setting them in concrete when you commit them to paper. Goals are also flexible. Things may happen that cause you to turn in an unexpected direction. When this happens, you can simply review and change your goals accordingly. Never let fear of goal setting stop you!

To establish your initial goals, get out that pen and paper and start figuring out just what it is you want to achieve with your new business. First of all, what is your ultimate target? Remember the vision we talked about in Chapter 10? That's your biggest goal of all, your mental picture of where you're going to be down the road. When you think big, you first imagine yourself enjoying the rewards of your success. You may picture yourself living in the house of your dreams, driving that expensive car you've always cherished, or visiting exotic countries that you've been yearning to see for years. You may see yourself behind a large desk with a magnificent view of the city, leading a meeting of your board of directors. You may think of the joy you will experience when you see your company's name on the *Fortune* 500 list for the first time. Think this is pointless fantasizing? Not at all! There is nothing wrong with envisioning yourself in the best of circumstances due to your ultimate success. As I told you before, your vision is the fuel that stokes your internal fire. Think big and you will achieve big!

In addition to your personal vision, you also have to establish a vision and a mission for your business. A *vision statement* is an idealized scenario of what your company can become—that is, a lofty image of the future. It is linked to your *mission statement,* which is more specific about what the purpose of the company is and where it fits into the bigger picture. An example of a vision statement might be: "To create joy and a spirit of cooperation among all children with our educational toys." Your mission statement is a more concrete set of goals that establishes what the company is specifically going to do; for example, "To provide the best in medical technology to doctors, hospitals, and laboratories."

Take a look at the commitment statement you developed

earlier and use it as the foundation for your own unique vision and mission statements. These are the advanced versions of the "reason to work" ideas you crafted not long ago.

Once you have established your vision and your mission, you can begin to focus on the long-term and short-term goals of your business—that is, the concrete results you are aiming for that will provide the yardstick to measure how well you are doing. Your long-term goals can be such things as achieving a certain sales figure within a certain time frame, acquiring a particular number of customers by such-and-such a date, or the position in the market you want to achieve by a specific month and year.

Your goals will have different schedules. If, for example, one of your long-term goals is to make $50,000 in sales your first year, your short-term goals will detail the steps you need to take to get there. These steps can and should be matched to time frames and should be quite specific about what you are going to achieve. "Increase my sales by twenty percent" is not quite enough. You need to specify exactly *how* you're going to increase your sales and the deadline you're giving yourself to do it; for example, "Sign up ten new customers by the end of June."

Whatever the goals you set for yourself, make sure they are goals you have a reasonable expectation of making. It's fine to shoot for the stars—but only if you can establish a realistic, workable plan that makes use of your available resources. (In Chapter 15 you'll learn some ways you can develop subgoals that help you do just this.) Conversely, you shouldn't make your goals too easy to attain. If you are hitting your targets month after month without much effort, then it's time to challenge yourself by setting higher goals.

Your goals should be directly relevant to what you are aiming to achieve. If a particular goal will do nothing to contribute to the ultimate success of your company, you need to reexamine it, and probably jettison that goal.

Flexibility is key to the whole process of goal setting. Changes in your industry or an unexpected turn of events can directly affect your goals and make it necessary for you to review and adjust them accordingly. You may also find your goals are simply not working the way you had hoped they would. If this happens, you will need to reexamine them or revise them until you find a formula that works for you.

Setting goals does not tie you down. Rather, it provides a guidance system for your ultimate success. As you establish and then achieve your goals, you need to be patient with yourself. I highly recommend that you keep a list of your goals in a visible place near your work area. This way you have a constant reminder of the targets you are shooting for and a means by which you can check your progress.

Chapter 15 provides a detailed analysis of how goals can be broken down into workable chunks. Before you start that chapter, though, I want you to take a very brief detour (Chapter 14) and learn about an important *daily* business safeguard you can (and should) build into your working day.

14

REVIEWING WHAT'S HAPPENING: BUILD QUIET TIME INTO YOUR DAY

Your business goals should inspire, excite, energize, and motivate you—but they shouldn't drive you crazy.

There's only one way I know of to keep them from driving you crazy, and that's the subject of this short chapter. *Once you set your goals*—whether they're to introduce a successful new product that no one in your industry has ever seen, or close eight new sales this quarter, or oversee a successful direct marketing campaign—*you cannot simply hack away at them without evaluating whether or not your efforts are moving you closer to or farther from them.* You must develop a real-world sense of exactly how your business efforts are working out.

It's easy to promise yourself that you're going to seriously review important new initiatives, but in my experience, there's only one tried-and-true method for *ensuring* that you gain the perspective you need to effectively evaluate your own work (and the work of others): Build quiet time into your day, every day.

You need time to sit quietly and think—time when the telephone won't ring, time when the radio or television won't be peppering you with advertisements, time when other people (be they family or business contacts) won't disturb you. You need time to silently ask yourself key questions:

- How is what I'm doing helping me to achieve my goal?
- How should I change what I'm doing?
- What new approaches should I be considering to attain this goal?

No advice on business strategy I can offer you will be as powerful and as effective as this: Make sure you take at least fifteen minutes, preferably thirty to forty-five minutes, of time for yourself, every business day. Don't talk during this time. Don't overschedule yourself, either. Simply sit quietly and ask yourself questions like the ones just outlined. Give yourself time to think about the way yesterday went, the way you'd like today to go, the position you'd like to be in tomorrow.

Take silent time for yourself by

- exercising in the early morning or late afternoon hours
- shutting off the radio during your morning drive
- arriving at your desk early and unplugging the phone
- taking an extended lunch hour that allows you to enjoy a quiet walk outdoors

Whatever you do to build quiet time into your day, *do it regularly*. Build a "safety valve" into your day that allows you the opportunity to step back, evaluate what's been happening in your business, and think about your goals in depth. If you deprive yourself of this essential self-management tool, I can pretty much guarantee you that your decisions won't be as effective as they should be.

If you can't give yourself fifteen minutes of silence a day to practice regular self-evaluation and business-evaluation routines, if you can't take a quarter of an hour to ask yourself key questions on a daily basis, then you're working too hard for your business's good! I know one entrepreneur who makes a point of briefly reminding himself, each and every day, of all his business's essential financial performance levels. He commits the key numbers to a business-card-size "report" every month and reviews them quietly for a few moments every morning!

So much for the foundation—quiet time. It's time to start looking at the structure of your goal-achievement system. In the next chapter, you'll learn how to develop and use your own personalized strategy map.

15

YOUR STRATEGY MAP

My wife, Anne, and I have been partners in our marriage, our lives, and our business for the last twenty-five years. And every single year we've written out our goals. We sit at the dining room table and ask ourselves, "What do we want to accomplish this year?"

We realized, after working together, that it was important to establish common goals so that we understood how we could work together to achieve them: what Anne's role was and what my role was. The fact that I'm able to write the number of books that I do, the fact that I travel nearly 250,000 miles a year, the fact that last year I gave 120 speeches is due in no small part to Anne's understanding that this allows us to accomplish the goals that we've set.

Our goals fall into three distinct categories, and the ones you developed on a preliminary basis in Chapter 13 should too. The three categories are immediate goals, intermediate goals, and ultimate goals. You should review the goals you set up in Chapter 13 now and determine which goals fall into which category, and you should review those goals on a daily basis.

On the mirror in my bathroom, there is a piece of paper that has the three critical questions on it: "What are my immediate goals? What are my intermediate goals? What are my ultimate goals?"

Years ago, a man by the name of Louis Bell, in Freeport, Maine, told me that that was the key to success—to focus on goals in those three categories. And to this day, when I shave, I ask myself those questions. What are my immediate goals? What are my intermediate goals? What are my ultimate goals? And, I always manage to keep the answers to those questions—which are the basis of my strategy map—in my head as well as on paper.

In our armoire, Anne and I have those goals posted. That's our basic strategy map. Each year we've written down what our immediate home-front goals are. In some cases they're as simple as buying a chair, getting a new dining room set, helping out our children with school problems, buying a coat—just a variety of things, and not that many. Those are immediate goals. The intermediate goals are longer term. What do we expect to accomplish during this year? Do we expect to take a vacation or are we going to skip it? Is it more important that we go to see Anne's mother in March and my mother in December? How are we going to schedule those trips? What do we have to do now to prepare for them? And then there are the ultimate goals: What is the bigger picture? What do we want to accomplish by the end of the year?

Anne and I realized that we had to agree on all of the goals, but there weren't hundreds of them. Many times the entire list was less than ten items long. You and I are not going to accomplish one hundred items in a given year. We would come up with a total of eight to twelve items—immediate, intermediate, and ultimate. Then we would post this list so that we would see it each day, and what we would do would be very simple. We would judge each and every day or each and every activity on the basis of whether or not it met the criteria we'd established. Could we afford to buy that chair if we ultimately wanted to take a vacation at the end of the year that would cost more money? Did we need that chair? Did we need that painting if it wasn't that important to us—and if it got in the way of a larger goal?

You're about to start a very exciting endeavor, that is, going into business. As the leader of your own business, you will be out there "slaying the dragon," and you will find plenty of dragons to slay. You do, however, need to be able to ask yourself, at any given encounter, "Does taking on this dragon move me closer to one of my immediate, intermediate, or ultimate goals?"

Make sure you choose what makes sense. When you've carefully laid out your goals, you have created a strategy map. Understand your goals. Make sure the immediate goals support the intermediate goals, and the intermediate goals support the ultimate goals. One way to make sure everything fits is to work backward from the ultimate goal (for example, develop $250,000 worth of business this year); ask yourself what you have to accomplish the first week, the second week, third week, fourth week, fifth week, and so on, to make that happen by week fifty-two.

Keeping notes about what you do is an important part of developing and updating your strategy map. When I first started DEI, I literally kept a daily diary of everything I did, and I rated everything according to a plus and minus system. Did what I spent my morning on move me closer to a particular goal, move me farther away from it, or have no impact whatsoever? I strongly suggest you take a similarly careful look at your own time for, say, five consecutive days. You'll learn a lot about where your time goes.

For my part, I discovered that I was spending less than fifty percent of my day actually doing business—doing the "right stuff" that moved me closer to my goals. I set a target for myself to spend seventy-five percent of my time focused on productive, moving-forward activity. That turned out to be a realistic target for me. My bet is that it's also realistic for you. (By the way, nobody manages to be productive one hundred percent of the time!)

Take a moment to formalize the goals you developed in Chapter 13 before you proceed to the next chapter. Identify the *ultimate goal* for your business this year. (It might be to close $250,000 in sales.) Identify appropriate *intermediate goals* for your business. (You might conclude that you'll have to sign contracts with one hundred $2,500 accounts over the next fifty-two weeks.) And finally, identify the *immediate goals* that will make those last two goals happen. (You might decide that you have to visit with five new contacts a week to turn an average of two of them into $2,500 customers.)

Customize the goals to suit *your* business, *your* industry, and *your* situation. Then write them down someplace where you can see them, day in and day out—that's your strategy map, your game plan. And of course, you'll want to review key questions daily by taking advantage of the quiet time discussed in Chapter 14.

Once you've established the goals and worked them through carefully, you must measure your progress each and every day. Monitor your own time—and perhaps even the time of others—ruthlessly so you can evaluate exactly how close your company is coming to hitting the goals you've established.

16

GETTING A FIX ON YOUR
IDEAL CUSTOMER

So, who's going to pay for your product or service? Whose life are you going to make easier, more enjoyable, or more profitable, simply by showing up for work each day? And if you sell your product or service to another business, it pays to know not only who your customer is, but who your customer's customer is.

Business-to-business marketing has become a fast-growing trend in recent years and is worth investigating if what you have to offer helps other businesses operate more profitably or efficiently. Indeed, many larger companies are hiring smaller independent firms and consultants to provide a range of services that saves them from having to hire employees to do the same job. It's this very trend that's making a great many small and midsize businesses profitable today. You could do worse than to target companies significantly larger than you are and find out what they're outsourcing and whether or not what you have to offer—such as contacts with temporary employees, proposal development, inbound telephone order–system arrangement, freelance design, production work—could be of interest to them.

Big companies are often interested in working with outsiders, even relatively small outsiders, because doing so entails far less financial risk than hiring and training (and supplying benefits to) a new employee. That's the good news. The bad news is, as I've already mentioned elsewhere in this book, companies in general, and large, prestigious companies in particular, tend to take a lot longer to pay their vendors than they would ever take to pay employees.

Customers Who Sell to Other Customers

You may be best served by selling your product, service, or solution to another company that has better distribution methods than you do for getting it out to end users. To judge this, you need to understand not only what your direct customers need, but also what their customers need. Your knowledge of the market and of what the distributing company is trying to achieve should help you to find ways to improve systems and services that will be beneficial and profitable to both parties. It's a win-win situation if the mix is right. The more you know about the market and the more information you have to work with, the better able you are to pinpoint your ideal customers and respond to their needs.

Low-Tech Research

If you're short on information about the kinds of companies you feel should be part of your prospective customer base, don't turn to expensive consultants or advisers (at least not yet). Go low-tech. Pick up the telephone and call purchasing managers (or whoever else would handle the decision to acquire your product or service) and ask for advice. Make it clear that the objective of your call is not to sell anything to anyone, but rather to get a clearer idea of how the company goes about selecting vendors in your field of interest. Explain that you're researching a new business venture and that you're trying to get expert advice about how business decisions are made in this area. Keep calling decision makers until you track down the information you need; keep calling until your work points you toward a number of likely customers; keep calling until you start to get a feel for the kinds of organizations you might end up doing business with. Then ask yourself, What do these groups have in common?

You may develop some good contacts for future sales efforts—and there's nothing wrong with that—but the point here is to identify the *profile* of your likely customers. What should you be looking for if you want to track down more customers like these? If you live and work in Chicago, and your focus is on delivering seminars that help organizations improve customer service, your profile of likely customers, developed after a week or so of persistent calling and interviewing, might look something like this:

> Organizations with a service focus, generating at least $15 million in annual revenue, employing at least one hundred full-time white-collar workers, within a three-hour drive of my Chicago office.

That's your likely customer's profile. That's the type of organization you're going to try to reach. That's the group that you've determined, through person-to-person contact, is most likely to benefit from what you have to offer. Is it possible that some organization in California with twenty white-collar employees and annual sales of $5 million could benefit from your program? Sure. But that organization is not your best bet. Remember, you're trying to identify what *likely* customers have in common.

If your customer is going to be an individual (perhaps one who will contact you via an 800 number to order a new piece of ski equipment, or one who will visit your restaurant because she loves sports-theme restaurants), it is incumbent upon you to go through the same "initial research" phase to find out who, exactly, is likely to purchase what you have to offer. Visit stores or malls or restaurants; find out who's patronizing the businesses that come closest to offering what you offer. Are your customers over age fifty-five? Under age fifty-five? Likely to purchase bargain merchandise? Likely to believe that "you get what you pay for"? Are they health enthusiasts? Couch potatoes? Single? Married? Parents? Kid-free? From a particular, narrowly defined geographic region? Evenly spread out throughout your proposed market area?

As in the situation where your target customer is an organization, you should try to find a way to initiate direct, person-to-person contact with particular consumers. Whenever you can, find an excuse to talk to the people who seem to represent your ideal customer. Ask them the key questions about price, performance, and promotion, or anything else that remains unresolved in your mind.

Write down what you hear. The answers you receive will help you focus in on how your product or service is designed or presented, and will also help you avoid expensive early mistakes. If you learn that your proposed restaurant site is considered dangerous or "too far out of the way" by members of the younger crowd likely to be interested in visiting restaurants with sports-related themes, then you'd better think twice before committing to that site!

17

"HELP! I NEED MONEY."

It's painful, but the truth is that many new businesses are going to fail within three to five years of start-up because they don't have enough money to keep going. *Undercapitalization* is perhaps the most common reason for failure. This catch-all term can encompass all manner of problems, from under-estimating your cash-flow requirements (perhaps because customers are paying more slowly than was anticipated), to shifts in the general economy that make your marketplace different overnight, to unexpected rises in the cost of raw materials you need to produce or prepare what you sell to others.

So, if undercapitalization is the big problem, where do you turn for capital? It may seem to logical that the first stop would be the bank, but this avenue has its problems. When it comes to small businesses, banks have generally been extremely cautious. They tend not to make loans that might be at above-average risk—and what is riskier than an unproven business just getting off the ground? Many new businesses, of course, are service-oriented, providing, say, mail-room management for midsize and large law firms. In such a business—or that of a consultant or a freelance designer or any of a hundred other similar undertakings—there's little or nothing for the bank to classify as "collateral." What, the bank will ask, can they repossess if the loan is not repaid?

If there is any doubt at all about your ability to repay the loan, the bank will more than likely turn you down. This is, unfortunately, particularly true for women entrepreneurs. Despite the (supposed) advances in gender relations during our enlightened age, women still have a much tougher time getting their foot in the door because of Stone Age preconceptions in many circles about the female ability to succeed in the male-dominated business world.

There is another reason why you might have trouble getting a loan from your bank. Small businesses are much more likely to request smaller loans than larger, more established organizations. To many banks, this would make loaning the money hardly worth their while, given all the paperwork, meetings, and follow-up that would have to be generated for a relatively small return on their loan. Look at it this way: The time, effort, and costs of processing a loan request are roughly the same for all borrowers, regardless of the size of their request. So it makes more sense for a bank to focus on processing the larger, multimillion-dollar loans—which carry significantly higher interest payments—than the $150,000 loan that a first-time entrepreneur might request.

Does all this mean that you shouldn't even bother with a bank if you're looking for a loan? Not at all! For one thing, slowly but surely, modern technology is changing the landscape of banking practices and making it increasingly likely that some banks will invest in businesses that many others wouldn't touch with a ten-foot pole. This is thanks to the banks' ability to access centralized data via computer networks, in particular, the sort of credit-scoring systems that credit card companies have been using for years. By using this data, bank loan officers are able to dramatically reduce the time and cost of processing a loan request, which makes an approval much more likely and timely for the small-business owner who needs money in a hurry. This technology also enables the bank to monitor loans in a more cost-effective manner. It's a more efficient system from which everybody stands to benefit.

Another development that favors small businesses is the current trend of larger corporations to rely less on bank loans for their own funding, thus increasing the interest of banks in lending to smaller companies. As a result, in recent years, many small-business owners have experienced increased success in obtaining loans. However, many others, particularly those in service-based areas, have found that the old prejudices still apply. Probably your best bet is to phone a few banks and test the waters yourself.

How do you know which banks to pick when applying for a loan? First, try to concentrate your efforts on the larger banks. You may think that you're more likely to receive individualized attention from a smaller bank, but in fact the larger ones are equipped to process your request more efficiently, in a shorter amount of time—and time is probably of the essence to your business! Second, before going to a bank, find out what they have to offer you in the way of products and services. If their borrowing options are restricted, with little to no flexibility on credit, then they are less likely to be interested in your small business. Third, ask what the typical loan-approval period is at that bank. If they promise you an answer within two days, they are more than likely going to be interested in your business. If it's going to take them two weeks, however, the chances are they're not in the small-business market and you'll want to consider talking to another bank. Finally, keep in mind that the size of your loan will affect the speed with which your request is processed. With or without an automated credit-scoring system, you should be prepared to provide lots of information about your company. (See Appendix A: "Your Formal Business Plan.")

There are two basic types of loans that you can get through a bank. The first is a *business loan* that is secured by either company or personal assets. In approving a business loan, the bank may require collateral from anybody who owns more than twenty percent of your company. Because of the risk they take in investing in your company, banks may call in your loan if your company shows any signs of floundering. Therefore, if the loan request is small enough, you may want to consider a *consumer loan* rather than a business loan. This would be, for example, a home-equity loan, mortgage or mortgage refinancing, personal loan, or no-income verification loan. As long as you have a healthy credit history and inform the bank that you intend to use the money for business purposes, your chances are good for obtaining the loan, and you run less risk of being required to pay back the money all at once if your business gets into trouble. However, bear in mind that some banks may not approve a personal loan for business purposes.

There are many other options that you can pursue besides approaching a banking institution. Many entrepreneurs start out by using their savings and/or borrowing money from family members or friends. In fact, historically about eighty percent of new business owners have started out by getting personal loans from people they know, rather than from financial institutions. The problems inherent in this approach are many and should be obvious. By borrowing money from a relative or friend, you run the risk of severely straining your personal relationship with that person, especially if the business doesn't do as well as you hoped and you are unable to pay back the loan.

If you decide to pursue this particular borrowing option, then do yourself a favor: Make it legal! *Never* borrow money from another person on a handshake alone. Unless you're dealing with somebody extraordinary who only wants to help and doesn't care about the return on the loan—and such a person is very rare!—you are far better off having everything down on paper so that the terms of the loan are thoroughly

understood by both parties and there can be no cause for disagreement or discord. Be sure that both you and the other
person sign your loan agreement, and have the document
witnessed and notarized. This is far better for everybody's
protection and will also ensure that you meet your obligation
to the lending party.

Whatever you do, try to borrow only from those people you
know can afford to lose their money if your company goes
under. You also want to ensure that your lender does not assume that because of his or her financial stake in your business, he or she can tell you how to run it. Your best bet as a
source for personal financing would be an acquaintance who
is looking to make an investment. Your accountant or attorney can probably recommend somebody, or you can spread
the word among your friends and colleagues that you are
looking for investors.

A valuable resource for small-business owners is the federal government's Small Business Administration (SBA),
which can act as both a lender and as a guarantor on loans.
SBA funds are provided only to start or build a business, not
for any other purposes, such as paying off investors. Your
business must meet certain guidelines set by the SBA. For
further information, call the SBA's Answer Desk at 800–827–
5722.

Two other governmental agencies to try are the Export-
Import Bank of the United States and the Office of Economic
Development (OED). The former is an independent federal
agency that provides financing and support to companies
within the United States that export goods and services. It
generally takes risks on companies that other banks pass up.
To learn more, call its hotline at 800–565–EXIM. The OED
operates at the state level to provide financing and help in
locating other sources for capital investments. Its programs
tend to change, but generally if your business will provide a
boost to a local economy (for example, an area where a major
employer has closed down), you are more likely to get finan-

cial help from the OED. Check with your local office for more information.

Another possible lender would be a *commercial finance company*. These companies generally assume the higher-risk loans that banks won't touch, which means that their rates and fees will be anywhere from two percent to ten percent higher than those at banks. This is a good avenue to explore if your company is growing faster than your loan ceiling, or you have a so-so credit history. This is also a good bet if you're looking to raise $500,000 or more.

Venture capital firms are another traditional option for small businesses looking for capital investments of $250,000 or more, up into the millions of dollars. Venture capitalists generally want to invest in companies that have the potential for fast and extraordinary expansion, a strong advantage over their competitors (for example, patents or other exclusive rights to a particular product or service), and a talented management team capable of handling explosive growth. These firms also tend to specialize in particular

- types of firms
- areas of the country
- industries

They may also have strict restrictions on the amount of money they will invest.

If you're looking for help from a venture capitalist, you should begin by sending an executive summary of your business plan to potential capital investors. If there is interest in what you have to offer, you will be asked for the entire plan. Beware of potential scams that will take money from you and give you nothing in return. There are those who pose as venture capitalists and will ask you for a fee or deposit "in good faith." If this happens to you—go running in the opposite direction! To find a legitimate venture capitalist, do your research thoroughly. Visit the library; call local business organizations or the Better Business Bureau to inquire about particular firms.

Many businesses receive financial help from investors called angels. These are wealthy people who are looking to make an investment that can potentially provide a higher return on their money than normal investments. Angels usually prefer companies that have good growth potential and strong management. Their investments are generally $200,000 or less, and they tend to focus on investments in their geographic region.

A unique option you might want to pursue is getting help from an angel network. A typical angel network is a nonprofit organization that will arrange to match wealthy investors with entrepreneurs who are looking for capital to either start up their businesses or keep them afloat. Generally, the business owner who is looking for help must first submit an executive summary outlining the history of the company, the background of the owner(s), and the company's financial needs. Once the proposal passes through the first stage of review, an invitation is extended to the entrepreneur to make a presentation at a meeting of the angel network involving potential investors for his or her offering. Normally, the entrepreneur has just ten minutes to make his or her case, so a good speaking ability is a must. Business plans and product samples should be brought along as handouts. (See Appendix A for detailed suggestions.) Interested investors will take and review the business plan and come to individual decisions as to whether or not to invest.

Angel networks can be a godsend for the typical entrepreneur who is looking for capital but has neither the resources to locate potential investors nor the time to present his or her idea on an individual-by-individual basis. These networks are also ideal for the investor who wants to put his or her money into a unique concept but doesn't know how to find it. By making it possible for these two parties to connect, angel networks create exciting business opportunities and save many small companies from going under. They also provide the foundation on which entrepreneur and investor can build a mutually beneficial relationship. There are often strict requirements for both entrepreneurs and investors who use an angel network. A fee of anywhere from $25 to $2,000 will be charged to you. Before pursuing this avenue, you will have to do a little homework. Guidance on finding an angel network can be obtained at your local library or through the Internet.

You may eventually find yourself being approached by a buyout group. If you're in a successful business niche, the competitors will soon come crawling out of the woodwork, and the pressure from them might make a buyout offer attractive to you. Being acquired by a larger company might also make it possible for you to reach a larger clientele and better serve both your customers and your employees. A buyout, then, may be another possibility for you to consider as your company grows beyond your financial means to sustain it.

Finally, there are the nontraditional means of financing your business. If the angels aren't there and you've exhausted all of the usual options, then you might want to consider some other avenues. For instance, you can sell your assets. You may have a car you can dispense with in favor of leasing a vehicle, or you may have a valuable item that will bring you a good amount of money. Selling your own property or investments may be one of your last-ditch efforts to save your business. You can also borrow money against your whole-life insurance policy (not term insurance). Many companies will allow you to borrow up to ninety percent of the cash value of your policy. There will be interest to pay, but not as much as you would pay with another option—cash advances on your credit card. Credit card debt can be extremely expensive and should be your final option when all else fails.

You can also employ a factor, that is, sell your receivables (the money you are owed) to a third party for cash, generally between fifty to ninety percent of the value of your receivables. The factor then collects the money due from your creditors and gives you the remaining value after all the money has been collected—and after he or she has deducted fees of anywhere from one to five percent of the original amount.

Finally, you can outsource your financing by using the services of a financial headhunter, who will find you investors in exchange for a commission on whatever capital is brought into your business. This option generally leaves you holding the short end of the stick, but is a good option for saving your company.

It takes work, time, and discipline—but with those in your favor, there's no reason you can't find financing arrangements that are right for your business.

18

"HELP! I NEED GOOD PEOPLE."

Do you ever! Part of setting up efficient systems in your new company is finding and hiring the right people to manage those systems for you—and then managing those people effectively. This isn't easy, especially when you have hundreds of other details to attend to and long, wearying hours of work, all of which leaves little time or energy to handle personnel issues.

But handle them you must. After all, you wouldn't be hiring people to work for you if you didn't need them. You couldn't possibly handle that entire workload alone; therefore it has become necessary to take on help. The first trick is to find and hire those employees—and they'd better be good, or you'll have a problem. If you hire somebody out of desperation and he or she turns out to be the wrong person, this can cost you more in money, time, and stress than if you had simply taken the time to do a patient and carefully considered search for the right individual.

You're going to start your search with one strike against you—the edge that the larger competition has. For an employee, there are several disadvantages to working for a smaller company, chief among them lower salaries and fewer benefits. It's simply more advantageous to a worker to go to a place that offers more to him or her personally. If you do find a winner for your company, the person may eventually be lured away to a bigger, better-paying corporation once he or she has been fully trained and gained useful expertise. It takes time and energy to find the right employees and get them trained, and you want to do what you can to retain them. So you have to find creative ways to beat out the competition who will try to steal your talent.

You can start by taking advantage of the fact that team spirit is a lot easier to generate in a smaller company than in a larger corporation—and this matters to people who want to make a difference in what they do. In fact, many people prefer to work in a small business because it gives them a greater sense of being part of a team—for that matter, they may feel like part of a family. Such people may also like the challenge of working for a company whose growth they can play a significant role in. Often, smaller businesses can also provide more flexible hours to employees, which is great for those who would feel more stifled in a rigid corporate environment or who simply need more flexibility. These are all factors that can provide important incentives when convincing somebody to come to work for you.

But how will you know when a particular person is the right one for you? You probably won't. Sometimes the people who impress us most at interviews are the ones who work out least well. They're great at selling themselves, not so great at doing the job. But you can hedge your bets by following these seven simple suggestions:

1. *Decide what kind of person you need.* Above and beyond everything else, you have to have a clear idea of what this employee is going to do and the results you will expect. Be

sure you put together a complete job description and the requirements for the position—for example, a college degree or experience in financial management. Remember—your best salesperson in the early stages is yourself!

2. *Use both traditional and nontraditional methods for getting the word out about your job opening.* Place ads in local newspapers and trade journals, and let customers and colleagues know that you are looking for somebody. Spread the word among all your contacts, including former coworkers and people in professional organizations. If the particular job is an entry-level position, you might also try posting it in college career offices. Sometimes you can find employees in the most unexpected places. It could be the person behind the counter at that sub shop or the concierge at a nearby hotel. If you notice qualities in others that you think fit the bill for the position you are looking to fill—for example, a strong work ethic, a good way with people, or a talent for numbers—then take a chance! Call that person in for an interview!

3. *Ask your employees for referrals.* If you can afford to, you might offer a bonus to any employee referring a new hire who works out. This involves your employees in the hiring process and adds to that overall feeling of teamwork.

4. *Use recruiters.* This can be an expensive option, but a recruiter can spare you a lot of legwork and may be more adept at locating the ideal candidate for your position, especially the management positions. He or she will also have greater resources and can save time by screening candidates for you.

5. *If you can't do it—hire a manager.* A manager can make life a whole lot easier for you by taking over tasks that you find too difficult or time-consuming—such as the hiring of new employees. Such a person can also manage other areas of the business for you, leaving you more time to focus on those areas you need or want to focus on.

6. *Always keep your options open.* Hold on to résumés and keep an eye out for good people. You may not be hiring at

the moment, but you never know when you're going to need somebody down the road.

7. *When interviewing job candidates, be sure to ask questions that are geared toward the qualifications you have established and your personal image of the best person for the job.* This may mean asking some pretty unconventional questions to assess characteristics that aren't immediately obvious on somebody's résumé. For example, you might ask a candidate about the risks he or she took on the last job, or under what circumstances he or she thinks it is proper to criticize the boss. Think of questions that pinpoint just what you want for the position and will elicit whether the person you're talking to meets those qualifications. This enables you to narrow your pool of candidates and zero in on just the right person. (Appendix B includes interview questions you can use to select the right person for the job.)

Once you've identified and hired somebody, how do you know you'll be able to keep him or her? You don't, of course, but you can offer incentives that may convince employees to stay with you for the long haul. For instance, if it's possible, you can offer stock options or profit sharing. This gives employees a stake in the company that more often than not inspires them to stick around.

Most important to keeping employees happy and committed to your company is making them feel that they are indeed part of your business family. Listen to them and provide guidance when it is sought. Talk to them about their problems and their career goals. Invite them to breakfast or lunch. On occasion, throw them a small party that allows them to kick back their heels and relax. Notice them when you pass in the hall, and call them by name. If your people feel that you genuinely care about them, they are more likely to be loyal and to want to sustain their employment with you.

And always remember to build on that cooperative attitude and sense of teamwork. Involve your employees in problem-solving activities—they may come up with creative solutions that save money or create sales. Take time to solicit their input, as well as to keep them informed about the latest developments. You do yourself a disservice if you isolate yourself from your employees. By being accessible to them and keeping them informed and involved, you will strengthen the chances of their remaining committed to you and to the company.

You have to develop a certain level of trust in your employees. One way of doing this is by delegating tasks—something which may be especially tough for you if you've gotten used to doing everything alone. But if you expect your business to grow, then you must grow with it, and that means giving up certain tasks and trusting other people to handle them for you.

And those other people have to trust you, too. You will probably walk a delicate tightrope when you delegate. You have to instruct, but not be overbearing. You have to monitor, but not hover. You have to judge the quality of their work, but not be overly harsh in your criticism. Most of all, you have to be a strong and fair leader.

What does it mean to be a leader? I've known many a business that has failed because the entrepreneur has failed to manage his or her staff well or to take advantage of the talents they have to offer. If you look at your employees as slave labor, there to do your bidding without question or even thinking, then there is not much point in hiring anybody at all. Your staff should provide additional opportunities to improve your business—that is, if you can truly lead them and make them a viable part of your team.

There is more of an art to leadership than you might expect. It is chiefly composed of four distinct qualities: vision, passion, communication, and discipline. You must first of all have a clear sense of direction or purpose to what you're doing. Your goals must be definable not only to yourself but to your employees. However, it is not enough for a leader to simply have a vision. There also needs to be a tangible sense of pride in the goals you are seeking to achieve and an honest desire to succeed. If you convey this to your employees, then you can inspire in them an equal passion for your goals and the belief that your shared goals can be achieved. Communication, though, is not a one-way street. You need to have the skills to communicate your vision to other members of your team, and you need to be open to receiving their input in return. Two-way communication is essential if you want to be an effective leader. And as an effective leader, you have to maintain discipline, both in yourself and in your team. The reins you hold need to be loose enough to allow your employees to share and communicate and be interactive members of your team, but tight enough to retain ultimate control of the direction your company takes.

As a leader, it is your job to enlist a cooperative attitude from all the members of your team, to involve them in your vision, to inspire and motivate them to achieve, and to influence them as the company grows and changes. This is quite different from being a manager, in which role you are more likely to simply implement the vision based on prescribed policies and procedures. A manager plans and organizes the work to be done. A leader creates an emotional response in his or her employees that inspires them to achieve the company's vision and mission.

But communication is probably the most important element of all in effective leadership. Without good communication skills, you cannot turn understanding of your mission into action. Proper, focused communication will serve to motivate and inspire your employees. It builds cooperation and trust. It keeps unforeseen issues from ballooning out of control. It resolves conflicts.

If you are a leader who can communicate well, you will be an effective problem-solver. Most of all, you will be able to establish a relationship with your employees that will ensure their loyalty and dedication, because you will have kept them informed and involved.

Finally, you should waste no opportunity to reward your employees for a job well done. From monetary incentives to an employee-of-the-month program, anything you can do that recognizes and applauds the superachieving employees in your company is a worthwhile investment. By doing so, you are guaranteeing that your workers feel noticed and appreciated—and they will appreciate you in return!

19

"HELP! I NEED MORE TIME."

Fact: A large portion of the small-business owners who fail do so because they are unable to manage their time effectively. Fact: There are twenty-four hours in a day, 168 hours in week. Fact: Any given day, you could have more hours of work to do than you have hours to work with. Fact: Organization and time management are crucial to your ultimate success, as well as to your mental health.

If you can't manage your time efficiently, you're not going to be able to manage anything efficiently. But if you're like most people, you probably find it very difficult to keep yourself organized so that you're always on top of things. It may, in fact, seem like an impossible dream to you. You've gotten so used to living with harried schedules and missed deadlines that you can't even imagine what a well-managed life could be like.

But proper time management and organizational skills can make all the difference to you as you cope with an unending workload of papers, meetings, and deadlines. Without developing these skills, you are doomed to day after day of dealing with one crisis after the next, which is no way to live. This is bound to have a negative effect on the health of both the company and yourself. Do you really want that?

Many people think they're too busy even to apply themselves to a new way of doing things. "Sure, it may be chaos, but I can't afford to learn a new system—there's no time." Nevertheless, it is possible to organize your business life so that you use your time more efficiently without sacrificing anything else in the process. Take a little extra time now to develop your time management skills, and you'll save yourself a lot of time in the long run!

To understand some of the different elements involved in time management and how best to tackle them, start by asking yourself a few questions. How do you begin each day? Do you always know exactly what you want to accomplish by day's end? Do you prioritize your tasks? Or do you tackle what's at the top of the pile—and hope for the best?

Organization begins right where you begin, when you get up in the morning. It does you no good to plunge into your work without some concrete idea of what you want to have done by the end of the day. Remember that goals are your road map to success—that's true even when it's your daily schedule. So begin each day by envisioning just where you want to be when the day is over. Create a strategy for how you will accomplish that goal. Before you sit down at your desk, decide what your priorities are and what you're going to do first. Then just do it. You can spend more time worrying about what needs to be done than it takes to just wade right in. If it helps, create hourly goals for yourself. That way if something happens to disrupt your schedule—as will inevitably happen—then you can just start again by establishing your goal for the next hour after you've handled the interruption.

How long is your typical workday? Do you manage to maintain the same basic hours on a daily basis? Do you consistently come in early or stay late, or put in twelve-hour workdays because you're having trouble keeping on top of it all? Or does the length of your workday depend on the amount of work you have to do at any given time?

Consistency is key to keeping everything balanced and manageable. So is knowing what hours of the day work best for you. You only hurt yourself if you push yourself too hard and take time away from your personal life in an attempt to catch up. Try to maintain consistent hours—particularly those hours in which you do your best work. If morning is a more productive time of day for you, then go into your office early and do what you can before the phone starts ringing, but leave at the same hour each day. This builds a stability into your routine that should help to keep you from feeling rushed all the time.

How well do you stick to a schedule? Do you write down a list of things you want to accomplish and keep to it, no matter what? Do you get distracted from your daily goals and end up with a number of unfinished items on your list at the end of the day? Or do you not maintain a list at all, just keep it all in your head and attend to matters as they arise?

Some people detest lists. They dislike having their lives dictated by items on a piece of paper. Yet without lists, what would we do? We can't remember every last thing we have to attend to, and priorities can get lost in a maze of paper. Lists provide a sense of direction to the goals we want to accomplish. So make your lists and do your best to stick to them as closely as possible. It gives a great sense of satisfaction when you tick off item after item!

What do you do when you have a number of projects all requiring attention at once? Do you put the least appealing projects to one side and focus only on the one that interests you? Do you attempt to work on the most difficult project, but then turn to the one that's easier? Or do you go a little crazy and make a mad effort to do all of them at once?

Once again, prioritizing is key. You can't get lazy and pick the project that's the most interesting or the easiest to do.

You have to choose the project that has the most immediate impact on your sales. The most important work gets done first. That is the most basic advice you can get from anybody. As you make that list of goals for the day, at the beginning should be your topmost priorities—that is, the projects that will do the most to create the sales you need to survive. The other stuff will still be there and will get done when it becomes a priority. It's okay to put it off until tomorrow if you really don't have to get it done today.

How do you handle deadlines? Are you fair to yourself and give yourself reasonable time frames in which to finish something? Do you tell other people they'll have something by Tuesday, when Thursday would do just as well? Or are you always underestimating how long it will take you to do something and then scrambling to meet your own deadline?

Deadlines are a fact of life in the business world. When you have a project, start by making an assessment of what it will take to finish it and the time it would take to do it if you had no other distractions to worry about. Then, since you will have distractions and administrative issues to address, add in an appropriate amount of time to account for your other business activities. (You might choose to add thirty to fifty percent more time, depending on your own situation.) From these elements, calculate the time you'll need to get it done, and then tack on a day or two for good measure. Be reasonable about what you can expect from yourself, given all that you have to do. If somebody is pestering you for a quicker turnaround and the project is something that really can't wait, then shift your other projects around to make more time—but only if it's necessary. By giving yourself adequate, reasonable time to complete a project, you feel a great sense of satisfaction when you can not only complete it on schedule, but even get it in early!

How do you end each day? Can you look back and safely say that you accomplished what you set out to accomplish? Did you finish most of what you had to do but still left some important tasks uncompleted? Or do you feel exhausted and frustrated because you worked so hard all day, yet there's still so much left to do?

It serves no purpose to punish yourself if you couldn't do everything you set out to do. Life is short, and you can't waste it fretting over lost accomplishments. Our days are filled to the brim with interruptions and events we can't always control. You have to accept that and move on to the next day's goals and activities—and learn from what didn't work yesterday.

Looking closely at your workload and how you organize it on a daily basis will tell you a lot about how you manage your time, and may provide some clues to how you can manage it better. There are some other shortcuts to success that you might want to consider. For instance, it's useful to keep a large calendar posted over or near your desk on which you can map out meetings, deadlines, road trips, and other obligations. This will help you better plan your daily activities because you can see at a glance what is due when, those periods of time when the crunch will be on for you, and those periods that you can devote to "catch-up" projects and activities.

Try to minimize the interruptions. If you have a deadline to meet, then don't answer the telephone; let your voice mail take care of the calls for you until you can return them later. If you need time to concentrate on a project, make it clear to others in the office that you can't be interrupted—but always let them know when you will be available again. If somebody barges in with a question or a problem that can wait, tell them so. Schedule regular meetings with your managers to take care of issues all at once, rather than piecemeal at times when you should be working on other things.

Also try to minimize the paperwork. This is not easy to do, but it's possible if you simply follow the golden rule of touching a piece of paper only once—twice at most. The more often you can attend to things when they come up, the more time you will have later, when that paper isn't there to bother you along with all the other papers you have allowed to accumulate. Furthermore, if that piece of paper has been hanging around for ages and has no obvious relevance to what you're doing—throw it out!

Finally, managing your environment contributes a lot to helping you to manage your time. Do what you can to organize your office so that it reflects order rather than chaos. Don't leave things on your desk that have no business being there. Put things away where they belong as soon as you've finished using them. Return files to their proper location; don't let them get lost in the piles on your credenza. Create a system that ensures that paper and information flow smoothly through the office. Make use of in baskets, out baskets, and (last but not least) trash baskets. One good tip is to create a "safe" trash basket, into which you put only paper, nothing else. Empty this basket once every few weeks. That way you may still be able to retrieve something that you need that may have been thrown out in error.

Organization requires maintenance, and that takes time. If you work alone, you have to do your own maintenance. If you can afford it, you should consider hiring yourself a secretary or office manager. If that's not in the budget this year, you will simply have to learn to be ruthless when it comes to prioritizing your own day!

20

DEALING WITH ATTORNEYS
(YOURS OR SOMEONE ELSE'S)

Sooner or later, it's going to happen: You're going to need legal advice. There's simply no avoiding legal matters when it comes to running a business. From preparing contracts to setting up partnerships and corporations, attorneys will most likely be an important part of your business's life. If you're lucky, you may need to call in a lawyer only occasionally. Nevertheless, it would benefit you greatly to be prepared and have one on call for when it's necessary.

There are any number of circumstances that may necessitate your calling in an attorney for assistance. You may need help understanding and complying with state or federal regulations that pertain to your business, or you may require assistance with the required paperwork when you decide to incorporate, or perhaps you need a review of a particularly daunting contract. Whatever your reasons, you should be very careful and extremely choosy when picking an attorney.

One of the best ways to find an attorney is to ask people

you trust for a referral. Talk to other business owners or perhaps to a loan officer at a nearby bank. Mention that you
want to find somebody with whom you can work comfortably, who understands your business well, and who won't
charge you $175 an hour to talk at length about the baseball
game he saw the night before. Your time, money, and attention are precious, and you won't want to spend a lot of valuable time educating a lawyer about the ins and outs of your
business. The right attorney should be familiar with the
workings of small businesses and the laws and regulations
that affect them. A past experience base that includes work
with firms your size is a good sign. The right attorney should
also understand your financial limitations. The right attorney
should be able to provide referrals to other professionals who
can help you, such as an accountant, without busting your
budget.

Be sure you understand your attorney's billing policies and
fees for services. For example, is there a charge for the initial
consultation? Does he or she charge for time spent on the
telephone? Is a different rate charged for work performed by
a researcher or paralegal? How will you be billed? This last
question is important. Most likely you will be billed on a
once-a-month basis. On rare occasions, an attorney will work
on retainer—that is, he or she will be available to perform a
prescribed set of duties, with extra fees built in for unexpected occasions such as a lawsuit or special project.

You probably don't need me to tell you that lawyers can be
quite expensive. So you should do what you can to save on
your legal costs by taking on as much of the work as you can
before bringing in an attorney. Do your own basic research
and make the phone calls that do not require a lawyer's review. You might choose to prepare initial drafts of contracts
and other paperwork yourself and ask your attorney to review them for you. Collect the documents you're going to
need and keep written records of all your legal transactions.
And be sure to attend every meeting with the lawyer fully prepared and organized! At anywhere up to $300 an hour in fees,

the clock is always ticking, and it is to your benefit to keep meetings short and to the point.

One of the most important jobs your attorney can do for you is to give you an estimate of the kinds of liability problems you may face in providing customers with your product or service. As I mentioned a little earlier in this book, the type of business structure you select for yourself can be a major issue here. If you're producing in-line skating equipment for consumers, your liability issues are going to be very different from those faced by someone who offers consulting on sales-training issues for businesses. Your attorney should be able to help you select the structure—corporation, partnership, sole proprietorship, S corporation—that makes the most sense for your situation. In addition, your attorney may be able to help you track down the right insurance provider, someone who can help your new business minimize the risks it may face in our ever-more-litigious society.

Speaking of lawsuits, what happens if someone threatens you with one? Well, the first thing to bear in mind is, saber rattling happens. Don't panic. I know of a literary agent who once received a threatening note from a business rival on a trivial dispute. It was a photocopy of a letter to an attorney, instructing the lawyer to take immediate legal action against my friend the literary agent. The idea was not to start a lawsuit, however, but to make my friend *think* that a lawsuit was in the offing. No such legal proceeding was ever initiated— because all that had been sent was that photocopy! The lawyer, it turned out, never received any communication whatsoever about the dispute.

I'm certainly not advising you to ignore any legal problem that comes your way, but I am suggesting that, sometimes, people make lots of noise about what they intend to do and then don't follow through. People have also been known to instruct attorneys to make lots of noise and then not follow through. The key is to keep your head, avoid getting spooked, and be careful about what you say. Don't volunteer information; don't make accusations; don't rehearse your version of events or try to win the other side's approval. Take your time. Don't let anyone define the terms of the dispute for you. Explain that you'll need to think carefully about the matter that's been raised.

While you may want to consult your own attorney to get advice on how to proceed in the face of a nasty letter or a threatening phone call from someone else's lawyer, you probably *won't* want to react by immediately instructing your lawyer to "hit back." Escalating these kinds of disputes without considering all the consequences can be a traumatic, time-consuming, and very expensive undertaking. Your time and energy need to go into building your business—not into venting your rage at a customer, former business partner, or supplier who's had the gall to hire an attorney or has threatened to do so.

When in doubt, remember this: Attorneys are used when people don't want to communicate with each other anymore. They're an (extremely expensive) alternative to rational discourse. If you listen patiently, carefully, and attentively to the concerns of the person who's trying to communicate with you, there's a very good chance you can avoid legal trouble altogether.

21

DEALING WITH BUSINESS RELATIONSHIPS THAT DON'T WORK

People problems. You can't avoid them. If everybody got along one hundred percent of the time, we'd find ourselves living in a perfect, but pretty boring, world. Just to keep us interested, though, problems can and do arise all the time— just as soon as a second person becomes involved, in fact. It may be your partner or an employee or a client or a vendor or a subcontractor or a distributor, or just about anyone else. Whoever it is, you're going to be dealing with personalities on a daily basis, and that means you will have to devote your time and energy to resolving interpersonal disputes.

Some of these disputes can be managed. In the case of others, you may decide, after fair and reasoned review, that the costs of maintaining an ongoing relationship with the person in question are just too high.

When you're running a business, you can't let the outside world determine where your energy is going to go. *You* have to decide what *you* want to focus on. And the sad truth is that there are some business relationships that are just too expensive—too much of a day-in, day-out drain on your energy—for you to continue investing in them. Some customers live to complain, in as time-consuming a way as possible, about every single aspect of the products or services you provide to them—and don't deliver one-twentieth of the revenue that would justify the time and effort you have to invest to keep these people on board. Some vendors will consistently deliver shoddy materials and services—and make you wonder how much money you're really saving by working with them. Some employees have a perfect genius for focusing on, and thus reinforcing, what *doesn't* work, rather than supplying what does.

If the vast majority of the business relationships you have experienced have had problems of this sort, then you may need to stop and reassess the way you interact with people or perhaps the way you select the people you're surrounding yourself with. But if only a *few* of your contacts are regular, persistent energy-sappers, you may rest assured that you live in the same world as the rest of us and are encountering one of its sad flaws: Some relationships just don't work out, as much as we might wish they would. When that happens, you have to find a way to extract yourself from the relationship—for your own sake and the sake of your business.

But how do you handle that problem, along with the thousands of other things you have to attend to? I've found that many people are afraid of confronting interrelational issues, no matter what their nature. They'd rather bury themselves in work than sort out a problem with another person or take any constructive action. This is too bad, because by allowing the problem to fester, they create negative conditions that affect both their own outlook on life and the quality of their work.

Denial, as the song says, is more than just the name of a river. It's a great way to avoid addressing potentially catastrophic problems in your business. Don't underestimate the amount of damage a dissatisfied, incompetent, or habitually negative person can do when he or she comes in contact with a key customer—or gets the urge for revenge—or decides, independently, to take on a "new challenge" within the organization that you'd rather have someone else tackle.

If you've decided that a customer *relationship simply isn't working out:* Explain what you've done in the past, outline what you'll be doing in the future, and thank the customer for his or her business. Then explain that time constraints make it impossible for you to handle one-on-one interactions in the way you have in the past, and ask forthrightly for the customer's support in this. If you can, and you feel comfortable doing so, you might point the customer toward an alternate source for the product or service he or she is trying to track down.

If you've decided that a vendor *relationship simply isn't working out:* Schedule a meeting with the vendor and explain that, for your next order, you're going to be evaluating other suppliers. You may want to leave open the possibility that the relationship could be resumed in the future, but be sure to specify exactly what technical, quality, or delivery problems you want to see resolved. (Many vendors will become extremely motivated after you break off the relationship and will move heaven and earth to resolve even long-standing problems. The prospect of winning a customer back can be an extremely powerful incentive.)

If you've decided that a relationship with an employee *simply isn't working out:* Schedule a private meeting at the *end* of the day. (Don't subject other people—or yourself—to the possibility that your employee might do something dramatic during the course of the working day.) Do not rehash old problems or assume a judgmental tone. Explain that you've spent a lot of time thinking about the person's relationship with your company, and that, having given the matter long and careful consideration, you've concluded that there simply isn't a good match. Compare the current situation to the task of trying to fit a square peg into a round hole. Make it clear that the decision is a difficult one for you, but make it clear that it is final. Then outline a clear next step for your employee to take (such as clearing out a desk or checking in with someone else in your organization about final paycheck arrangements).

A word to the wise: When you're just getting started with your business, you can avoid virtually all personnel crises related to clerical and administrative work by signing on with a temporary employment service. These services can provide you with a steady flow of workers, each of whom will have to be trained in the procedure in question. On the downside: Good people tend to move on to other assignments or receive full-time job offers. On the upside: The situation is just as flexible as you need it to be, and you don't have to continue an assignment with an employee who doesn't suit your needs—or feel terrible about summoning someone else from the pool of workers.

PART III

FINDING OUT

Is it working? And what will you do if it isn't?

The reality of the marketplace can be a daunting experience. I remember once sitting in a prospect's office; this person, whom I had thought was about to agree to a program, had just said to me that he was going to "think about" our discussion. We had settled on the dollar figures, everything had come together, and I thought I would close the sale. Then he said he'd think about it and let me know.

If all went my way and we got this project, it would probably be three months before we started it. I was sitting there across the desk knowing that I needed this particular piece of business. In fact, I needed it desperately in order to pay the rent, and if I could just get ten percent of that down payment during that meeting, I would have it made. But my contact wasn't ready to make a commitment; he needed to "think about" my proposal. I had to sit there and, as the expression goes, not show the sweat. It was one of the most difficult moments I ever faced, because I couldn't say to him, "I need this money now"—even though I wanted to. If I'd done that, I would have lost all credibility—and I certainly would have lost the sale.

My company made it through the month; I was able to secure other financing to see us through. But that sales call had been a heart-stopping experience. I think every entrepreneur has one or two moments like that. In this part of the book, though, you'll learn how to keep such crises from happening any more often than is absolutely necessary.

22

MARKETING: WHY PEOPLE BUY

Human beings like to think they are rational creatures, but in fact the opposite is true. We make decisions, run our lives, develop our purchasing patterns, choose an investment counselor, or hire a fashion consultant primarily on the basis of some internal hunch, some gut feeling. "Wow," we say. "That's just what I want to look like." Or "Boy, if I bought such-and-such, I could stop worrying about . . ." Then we confirm our decisions with rational analysis or on the basis of a set of recommendations or letters of endorsement or some other kind of authoritative backing, and tell ourselves we're being oh-so-reasonable. But marketers know that at the end of the day, the "gut feeling" is what counts.

Let's say I've been thinking about getting a new car, something a little bit jazzier than the old station wagon this time, something that will give me a feeling of adventure. Suddenly, every time I pick up a magazine or turn on the television, I'm noticing car ads. Not all car ads. Minivans, for example, I

screen out completely. I'm not looking for safety and reliabil-
ity, and I don't need enough passenger seating for an entire
soccer team. I want something with fast acceleration, something that handles curves, something that might even turn a
few heads when I pass. When I come across an ad for a car
like that in an ad, instinctively I pause, and my pulse picks
up a notch: I'm imagining myself behind the wheel. A few
moments later, I look to see what the price tag is, and turn
the page. Dream on, I say to myself. One of these days,
though, the price will be right, or almost right, or I'll get a
raise at work. Something will give me the little push that's
going to get me to buy, and my decision may not be entirely
rational. The truth is, in this case, my desire for adventure is
stronger than my need to do the sensible thing one hundred
percent of the time.

Most marketing is emotion-driven. Television advertising,
for example, is virtually all based on emotional appeals.
Whether the product or service being advertised is fast food,
a new phone service, or a chain of copy stores, the appeal is
to some gut feeling, like hunger or fear or desire or insecurity.
The next time you're watching television, ask yourself if the
ads you're watching are really about instant coffee, deodor-
ant, tires, or toothpaste—or are they about our desire to be
part of the "in" crowd, to avoid embarrassment, to be safe
and secure, to hook up with a member of the opposite sex?
How many beer commercials aimed at males, for instance,
seem to be sending the message that the more beer you drink,
the more attractive you'll be to women? Talk about a dubious
proposition!

The truth is that the concepts we attach to certain products
and services don't have to make sense on a rational level to
be successful. They just need to pack a punch.

I'm not saying human reason has no role to play in decision
making. Most of the time the rational mind plays the heavy
pretty well, stepping in before we buy and insisting on performing a sort of "go" or "no go" check, to prevent us from
doing something really foolish. On a day-to-day basis, how-

ever, most of us make our decisions for emotional reasons, and most of us find ourselves attracted to situations that fill strong emotional needs. Our powers of logic serve mainly to confirm the soundness of positions that we assumed instinctively or because of some strong emotional need. Of course, we might not ever admit this to ourselves, because, as I noted earlier, human beings like to think of themselves as rational creatures.

You can see where this is going. The fundamentally emotional drive behind people's buying decisions has endless ramifications for your business. When you're thinking about how to market a product or service, you need to figure out how to elicit strong emotional responses, and then how to follow up with the material people need for an intellectual confirmation. Simply citing facts and figures isn't going to be enough. People have to *want* first, and then they have to give themselves *permission*. Are you sure you're covered in both these areas?

Maslow's Hierarchy of Needs

You may remember reading the work of Dr. Abraham H. Maslow at some point in college or high school. He was an American psychologist (1908–1970) whose incredibly influential theory of the "hierarchy of needs" has helped shape not only psychology but marketing as well.

Maslow's basic premise was very simple. People have all kinds of needs. Some needs are more fundamental than others, but all are important. If one level of needs gets met, people instinctively move on to satisfying the next need level.

To illustrate his theory, Maslow drew a pyramid with five horizontal sections—five levels of needs that must be satisfied from the bottom up. The first level has to be satisfied, in other words, before the individual can move on to the second, and so on.

At the lowest level Maslow placed basic survival needs like food and water. The second level was the need for safety and protection, such as clothing, housing, safety and security systems. Once safety and survival are taken care of, said Maslow, humans go on to seek love and belonging, the third level of need: friendship, companionship, membership in social groups. The fourth level is the need for self-esteem. This has to do with the desire to be recognized by others for your qualities and abilities—to develop a healthy sense of self-respect. The fifth and final level is the need for self-actualization. When the other four levels of needs have been taken care of, we still feel driven to fulfill our own inner capabilities, to reach personal goals and develop over time.

All of us have all of these drives in different degrees. The point is that at any given time, anyone you talk to is going to be working on fulfilling one or more of the five basic drives. If it's one-thirty and you're meeting with a prospect who hasn't eaten lunch yet, you might want to address the first level first—that is, if you want the person's undivided atten-

EXHIBIT 5

Maslow's Hierarchy of Needs

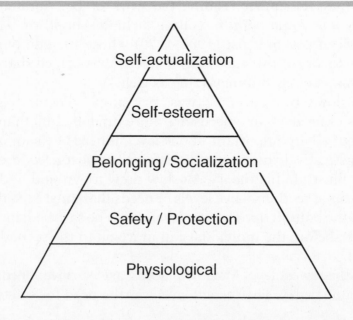

- Self-actualization
- Self-esteem
- Belonging / Socialization
- Safety / Protection
- Physiological

tion. If your prospect has had lunch but is facing a serious financial crisis, on the other hand, you may want to appeal to the need for safety: How can your product or service be used to protect the person's family, ward off poverty, and the like? If it's insurance you're selling, address ways to provide for the kids in the event of the prospect's death.

The parent facing financial difficulties has a very different motivation from that of the single person considering, say, a climb up Mount Everest. The Everest ascent probably falls into the very top category, self-actualization. The climber is seeking a sense of personal accomplishment; at least, it's hard to imagine any other reason for taking on such an arduous assignment. It's no use appealing to the worried parent's desire for self-fulfillment, or to the mountain climber's desire for safety and security. The parent does ultimately seek self-fulfillment, in the grand scheme of things, and the climber wants to live long and die peacefully, but these motivations are not foremost for them at this time. Check back in five years and the picture may look different.

By studying Maslow's pyramid and learning to apply it to the marketing task, you'll become a better spokesperson for your business. Why? Because you'll understand your customers better. You'll know how to respond to them more effectively. With a bit of practice, you should be able to make a more or less instant best guess at what is guiding your target customer at the moment, and how what you offer can address that person's key concerns in one or more of the five categories. Once you've learned how to do this, your time will be spent more effectively, and so will the customer's.

The first step, then, is to take a good look at your product or service and figure out what it does for people. What driving motivation is it designed to satisfy? The more urgent the motivation, the more emotional urgency you can tap into in your marketing. Maybe your product satisfies at more than one level. Maybe the car you're selling is not only sporty but comparatively inexpensive, and therefore attractive to those who can't quite bring themselves to spend the kids' college fund on a new automobile. Smart marketing gets an emotional foot in the door and then appeals to the final decision maker, the consumer's reasonable side. Once you've figured out how to do those two things, you're way ahead of the game.

Sit down with Maslow's pyramid of needs and figure out where your product or service fits. Take some notes. If you can't come up with a need it meets, you may want to reevaluate how you're presenting your product or service—or even the essentials of the product or service itself. If you don't think of something right away, don't despair. Sit down with some prospective customers and do a little informal market research. Find out what driving motivation appears to be guiding them. Once you tap into the force that's driving your customers at a fundamental level, you'll be well on your way to identifying a marketing or sales strategy that makes sense for your business.

23

CUSTOMERS MUST DRIVE
THE PROCESS

Reality. Why does that word often carry such depressing connotations? As in, "I think Melanie just got a major dose of reality." Translation: Unexpected cost overruns have derailed Melanie's project after only three weeks.

Reality isn't such a bad thing, really. But it can and will bring disappointments and surprises. The parts aren't available. The landlord is talking about hiking your rent. White sneakers just went out of style. The best plan in the world won't anticipate everything that could go wrong—or unexpectedly right! That means you have to plan for what you can't plan. You have to monitor your goals, evaluate your progress, make adjustments. Most of all, you need to stay in touch with your customers.

One of the most common mistakes entrepreneurs make is spending a lot of time putting together what seems like a foolproof business plan, and then sticking to it too rigidly. It's understandable, but it can also be fatal. Remember this: A plan is only a plan until it's put into practice. Then it becomes something else, something dynamic and changeable.

A potter makes a teapot. First he throws the clay on a potter's wheel, then he shapes it, then he fires it, and finally he glazes it. Is it a teapot yet? Not quite. Not until he fills it with tea and pours. If the spout isn't quite right, the tea will go all over the place instead of into the cup. If the lid isn't right, it may fall off when the pot is tipped. And the handle may get too hot to hold when the pot is full of tea. He needs to do some fine-tuning before his teapots are perfect and ready for the marketplace.

A good potter won't be discouraged by these early disappointments. He knows he's learning. Let's say he gets the design just right, but he goes with a glaze that his customers aren't crazy about. This is where the potter shows his business instincts. He listens to what his customers are saying. "Have you got a teapot in pale green to match these cups?" "I'm looking for one that's about half this size." He asks questions, engages the customers in conversations about what they want. Then he makes adjustments.

You can't rest on a good plan, no matter how much research went into creating it, no matter how many experts swear it will work. After all, the plan isn't going to pay your bills: Customers are. And if the plan turns out not to work as well as you thought it would, they won't be doing it for very long.

This goes for any new venture. Before you commit costly resources to a marketing plan the "experts" say will work, test it out. Get in front of some prospective customers and do a little instant field research. Don't try to sell your product or service, but do ask for input and opinions. Do the prospective customers you're interviewing seem interested? Excited? Lukewarm? Explore with them the reasons for the reactions they're sharing with you, and use that information to fine-tune your product or service.

You will know your product plan is ready when your prospective customers—who have agreed only to offer insight and advice to help you fine-tune what you're offering—start to say things like, "How do I sign up?" "When will this be available?" "Have you got any openings next week?" That's the magic moment you're waiting for, the "expert advice" you've been waiting to hear. Don't rush to commit yourself to any marketing plan before that point!

Your customers (if you have them) or prospective customers (if you're just starting out) know more than the experts about what they like and don't like, what they need and don't need, and they're usually only too happy to talk with you. Take advantage of their input!

Find out what people think. Show them the print ad you're planning to run or the sample product you're about to start passing out during your face-to-face meetings. Does what you've put together genuinely pique their interest? If not, why not? Make a point of pursuing any negative comments to their source—ask the interviewees to be ruthless with you. Leave yourself open to criticism, and don't let yourself get defensive. It's easy to have strong "parental" feelings about your ad (or whatever the project is), but your opinion isn't the one that counts here. Which would you rather deal with— some constructive criticism from a potential customer who represents thousands of *other* prospective customers, or a huge expenditure on a major marketing campaign that is fatally flawed? Your job is to listen, learn, and improve, and you can do that only by spending time with your customers face to face and finding out what they're really about.

Whether it's a new product, a new print-advertising campaign, a new Web site, or a new retail location, you need to be in tune with your customers—not with some smooth-talking ad salesman or the proponent of a one-size-fits-all promotion campaign designed to meet the needs of businesses "just like yours." These sources may or may not be acquainted with the issues your customers face on a daily basis. In all too many cases, ad salespeople and other promotional experts are acquainted only with their own sales quota requirements. I've met far too many entrepreneurs who have laid down sizable "investments" for elaborate and expensive print or broadcast campaigns that were totally mistargeted.

Whether the people you're speaking to respond positively or negatively, you will want to zero in on what they're reacting to. Was it content, for example, or presentation? Certain key customer groups will have strong reactions to the *way* you present information, and you'll want to find out as much about these prejudices as you possibly can.

Many years ago, when I was still fairly new to sales, I was working for a video retailing company that specialized in producing television commercials for retail stores. I had a big presentation coming up at a major retail manufacturing company, and of course, I had researched the company to death and felt I knew "just what they needed." I was determined to wow the executives of this firm. I was so determined, in fact, that I actually went out and hired an artist to put together a flip-chart presentation. I had never done that before. So I went in and made my flip-chart presentation to the senior vice president of retail about why he should be on television, and I have to say, it was a great presentation. It looked fantastic. Finally I got done flipping through those pages, about fifteen of them, and I was really proud of myself. The senior vice president of retail turned to me. "God, I hate flip-chart presentations," he said. That was the end of the meeting!

I learned a lot from that experience. I learned that, in my business, people are interested in me—the person who's going to be doing the training. They want to see how I interact with people, what new ideas I bring, what speaking skills I offer, how persuasive I am during the meeting. They don't want to focus on flip charts. They want to be convinced that I can turn their salespeople around! As you can guess, I haven't made the mistake of relying on an elaborate series of color flip charts since that experience.

To learn what you need to know, you can't stay at home. You've got to make appointments. Even a single appointment can teach you a lot. That flip-chart experience wasn't wasted time, on the contrary. Mortification is a great teacher. All firsthand experience is a great teacher. Sure, appointments are for selling; but just as important, they are your chance to listen, ask questions, and practice your skills.

Your customers and prospective customers have the information you need, information that can make or break your business. You can learn a lot from experts, but customers are by far the best teachers, because they will tell you about your service, your product, your presentation. They'll tell you, in one way or another, about your particular business solutions: the strengths, the weaknesses, the possibilities for improvement.

You'll get the most benefit from such experience if you follow it up with some analysis. Say you've been on a sales call. If you were a member of a sales force, you'd sit down with your manager and talk over the meeting. You probably don't have that luxury, but that shouldn't stop you from being your own manager. A friend of mine who runs a business sits down and analyzes every sales call he makes. He works off a checklist, noting down what he did well and what he did less well. He also keeps a list of frequently asked questions and questions that he wants to ask, and he rehearses possible responses. This kind of review is not hard, and it works.

After all, business relationships are like any other kind of relationship. They depend on certain basics, such as good communication, mutuality, responsiveness, and fair dealing. As a businessperson, you want to sell something people need. And people want to buy things that are going to help them—or maybe just make their lives a little more pleasant. A relationship is working well when both parties are benefiting.

So that's the message of this chapter. Get out there and meet people before you commit to that snazzy advertising campaign. Engage them in conversation; test out your ideas; make mistakes on a small scale so you don't have to make them on a large scale. Get person-to-person feedback before you commit valuable resources. Whether you're talking to prospects, recent customers, long-term customers, or people who fit your customer profile and are willing to critique your product or service (or your presentation of it), you need to be in touch with the people on the front line—and you need to listen to what they tell you.

At DEI we have this saying: Fit the product to the customer, not the customer to the product.

Too often salespeople are so involved in trying to make the sale that they fail to realize that the sale is not the issue. As we've seen, the issue is what the customers do, how they do it, and how you can help them do what they do better.

The business owner has to say to himself, "How does my product or service fit what the person that I'm talking to does?" Not the other way around. Too many salespeople begin by doing what we call a product dump. That is, they simply try to fit their product to the company, instead of understanding what the company's doing and making the product work for them.

The successful business owner is aware of product malleability. *Product malleability* is a term that describes the way I adapt my product or service to help those people that I'm working with. It's more than product knowledge. It's really adaptability. And adaptability and change are really what make for a successful sale. Product malleability also comes into play when you apply your product or service to new circumstances. How else can others use what you have to offer in their current operations? Arm and Hammer has been selling baking soda for years on the premise that in addition to acting as an ingredient in food, their product also freshens up refrigerators and helps keep them odor-free. Now, there are people, like me, who do no baking whatsoever, but who buy the product solely to keep the refrigerator smelling nice! Is there a similar extension of your product or service that you should be considering?

So—don't try to fit your product or service into what the customers do. Instead, find out what they do and learn how you can match what you offer to that situation.

24

GOING DIRECTLY TO
THE CUSTOMER

Today, mail order is a huge and rapidly growing segment of the economy. Some like to think of direct mail as the on-paper equivalent of telephone sales. For some business ideas, like magazines and certain gift items, mail order is the perfect forum.

Why are a lot of small-business people interested in direct mail and other mail-order-selling strategies? One big reason is overhead. Compared to a retail operation, there's no storefront to maintain, fewer problems regarding inventory management, and possibly no commuting costs or child-care costs. For some businesses, there are definite advantages to a direct-mail campaign. It's totally under your control, and once you've developed a formula that works, you can expand it as you see fit.

Direct mail is based on a few simple principles:

- Focus
- Promotion
- Testing

Focus is what makes direct mail practical. The success of a mail-order campaign almost always depends on targeting. You probably can't afford to send a promotional mailing to every household in America, and you probably don't want to. You want to get the most "bang for your buck." The secret of success in direct mail lies in highly specialized lists: lists of people who buy luxury goods, lists of people who like gardening, lists of people who have purchased vitamins by mail within the last ninety days. Customized lists allow you to zero in on people with specific buying behavior, raising your rate of return dramatically. Sure, you could send out a mailing to everyone in a certain zip code, and you might do pretty well, if you know how to pick your area. The more specialized your list, however, the higher the rate of response, which means you get the same return or better with a smaller investment. Lists are to direct mail what territory is to sales and what location is to the restaurant trade. Which is to say, everything.

There's a catch, of course. These lists can be expensive. The more specific the list, the more it will cost. List brokerage is a thriving industry in itself these days. Check a good metropolitan Yellow Pages under "Mailing Lists," and you should find plenty of companies that specialize in just this. After the basic list selection questions have been addressed, small-business owners who can afford to do so, however, may prefer to hire someone on a temporary basis to coordinate mailings. It's a time-consuming job, and many businesspeople already have enough to do.

The second basic component of direct mail is promotion. Here I suggest that you not try to reinvent the wheel. Get hold of a direct-mail piece that's working, something advertising a product or service that's similar to yours, and adapt it. Be a shameless copycat. That direct-mail piece, if it was sent by a large company, has been the subject of tens or even hundreds of thousands of dollars' worth of research—millions, in some cases. Put that research to work for you. Study the layout. Check out what benefits are being advertised and what's being done to promote the product. Then go forth and do likewise. Design your own mail piece based on the best elements of the campaigns that most closely resemble what you're trying to accomplish.

Remember, you need to include some kind of an offer with a direct-mail piece. You want a perfect stranger to fill out your coupon and pop it back in the mail. That means you'll need to offer an incentive—a free sample of your product, say, or thirty days' free service, or fifty percent off a special item. Take careful note of the offers included in the direct-mail pieces you study.

It's also smart to test the market before mailing to an entire list. Don't bet everything on a piece (or, even more risky, an expensive multipage catalog) unless you're darned sure it works and that it makes economic sense for you! Start with a three-thousand-to-five-thousand-piece mailing using your basic design and demographic mailing strategy, and see how it does. In subsequent mailings, keep tweaking the piece to see if you can get better results; for example, try altering the offer slightly in a third of the run, and then compare the results to determine which version of your mailing piece draws a higher response rate, and then go with that. Keep track by coding the coupons, and continue to experiment, monitoring which piece is pulling best.

Mailing costs and procedures are complicated and can be expensive, but there are substantial discounts available for those who can manage to make sense of the intricate and complex regulations administered by the U.S. Postal Service. Again, if you can afford to hire a professional—someone with a postal permit and the necessary software, someone who can provide mailing services and track down the lowest possible rates for you—it's probably going to be worth your while to do so. A good relationship with someone who knows the ins and outs of mail classification will significantly enhance your chances of success.

A good, reliable printer is a necessity. Try to find someone who can turn around your mailing on time and on budget.

You'll be depending on this person's services a great deal, both in the early testing phase and later on, when it's time to roll your mailing out to a wider audience. There's nothing more humbling than realizing that the big mailing you're basing your next quarter's income on is illegible because your printer substituted a new color without your authorization!

Good direct-mail pieces usually

- are focused around a letter that makes a direct appeal to the reader
- feature a "grabber" sentence in the very opening paragraph
- use simple, accessible, friendly language
- use a P.S. that focuses on a compelling benefit provided by what you have to offer
- offer the reader a clear, understandable "next step" (for example, a postpaid card to return)
- create attention, interest, desire, and action
- use a black Courier typeface (the kind that resembles typewriter print) on white paper, and employ accent colors carefully
- include a simple, easy-to-understand response form
- tie the benefit (a discount, say) to action by a certain time (for example, "You must return the enclosed form to us by March 1 to take advantage of this special offer!")
- use short paragraphs
- are addressed to a single, distinctive reader—not the world at large

In addition to direct mail, you may want to consider mail-order arrangements based on promotions and advertising that appear in magazines, journals, newspapers, or even over the Internet. Many of the same guidelines apply to these advertisements, particularly the "grabber" rule and the need for a clear next step for the reader to take.

In these situations, your selection of an advertising medium—for example, a popular gardening monthly, a respected industry trade magazine, the sports section of a major newspaper, or a popular Web site devoted to a certain rock band—will serve the same function as the list you buy in a direct-mail setting. These advertising sources should be selected (and tested) with great care. Assuming that your offering will be of interest to "the general public" is a classic, and usually fatal, mistake. Find the medium that precisely targets the group most likely to react positively to what you have to offer, and then monitor your promotional efforts closely to determine what has worked and what hasn't.

In either setting—direct mail or advertisements that encourage readers to contact you directly—you may opt to offer customers and potential customers access to a toll-free 800 or 888 number for easy ordering. Just be sure you're prepared to man the lines yourself or to secure the services of someone else who can before you start circulating the number. If a customer calls in from another time zone at an inconvenient time to discuss a shipment that went awry, will she be forced to leave a message on an answering machine? These days, there are outsourcing firms that can help you manage incoming toll-free traffic for a price; this option may make the most sense for some entrepreneurs, but the budget figures can be daunting, so make sure you get information on all the costs involved before you commit to any company for this service.

25

THE ADVERTISING AGENCY TRAP

This is a short chapter because its message is straightforward: For most beginning entrepreneurs, relying on an advertising agency to track down customers is a big mistake.

Why? Let me count the ways. Advertising agencies cost money, sometimes a lot of money, and that's a critical resource as a business is starting up. Advertising agencies often make promises they can't keep, and that's a problem that can cost you both time and money. And finally, and most important, advertising agencies insulate you from the process of identifying your market on a face-to-face, one-on-one basis.

There may well come a time when you decide that to expand your business, it makes sense to secure the services of a qualified advertising firm that has ample experience in working with your type of business. But in the vast majority of cases, it's a mistake for you to do so in the first year or two of your business. You have to use that time to set up your own relationships with customers and to begin to do something no advertising agency can do for you, which is move toward a partnership relationship with your key accounts.

What is a "partnership relationship"? Well, there are four levels of selling that you'll go through with your customers. The first is that of the seller—that is, where you are selling to an individual and there is nothing more than a dollar transaction. The second level is that of a supplier, where you're supplying information or your service and there is some degree of relationship there, but it's minimal. The third is the level of the vendor, and that's probably as high as you're going to get in the opening years of your business relationship with any customer. When you're a vendor, you have a relationship of significant trust and honesty, where you're doing business for the person. I would say that the vendor relationship usually takes a year or two to unfold. When it does, you know, at least, that if the company is going to stop buying from you, they're going to call you first and let you know.

The important point is, though, that you can't get to the fourth level without having done the work to get to the third level! The fourth level, which is the most difficult one, is that of the partner. A partnership is a situation of mutual dependence; you need them and they need you. Your expertise is expected and appreciated; you know what they're planning and where they're going to be and how you fit into that picture in the short term and the long term.

First-time entrepreneurs often have the illusion that an advertising agency can "deliver customers." Often, they're wrong, but even when they're not, they miss out on the opportunity to begin building toward those all-important partnership relationships with key customers. *You* have to be the one who identifies key customers and builds the relationship through the four stages. Imagining that you can delegate that task to someone else or perform it yourself before you've learned firsthand about what does and doesn't work for your customers is a classic early mistake. Don't lose the time or the money. Make the job of tracking down customers during your first few years *your* job, and make sure *you're* the one who learns the key lessons on relationship-building within your business.

26

THE DAILY-CALL ROUTINE

The legendary Hollywood agent Swifty Lazar supposedly kept a sign in his office that read: "Make something happen before lunch." If I had to summarize, in a single sentence, the philosophy necessary to turn your start-up into a successful operation, Lazar's advice would probably come closest to the mark.

You're the person who has to make something happen before lunch. In the vast majority of cases, the head of the business—or one of the two heads of the business, in the case of a partnership—is the very best person to do the one-on-one selling. Not an outside salesperson. Not an independent sales rep who handles fifteen other clients. You.

In this chapter and the ones that follow, you'll see how to turn the ideal of personal sales into a reality. All the advice that follows on sales strategy assumes that you or your partner is assuming, at least in the early stages, the role of the salesperson for your organization—the person responsible for prospecting, developing new business. In most cases, that prospecting work is best accomplished through the simple act of picking up the telephone and talking to people about what you can offer them. That all sounds fine in theory—but how, exactly, are you going to make something happen before lunch, day in and day out?

The answer is, you're going to develop a basic prospecting script that you can use to make a certain number of phone calls each and every day. And you're going to develop that "calling muscle" by keeping at your calling routine, no matter what. By making a commitment to basic prospecting each and every day—typically, making between ten and twenty-five calls per day—you will also be taking out an "insurance policy" against future income problems.

Many beginning entrepreneurs make the mistake of assuming that they can put off daily prospecting work. The typical pattern that develops when people are running their own business, especially if it's a one-person business, is a roller-coaster effect: They go up and down and up and down and up and down; a few good months are followed by a few terrifying months, followed by a few good months, and so on. Those peaks represent high points in income, where people relax and assume that since all is well and they have enough customers now, they don't need to worry too much about finding new business. And then key clients vanish—their needs change or competitors snap them up—and the income starts to dip, and then down at the bottom there's a crisis, and all of a sudden prospecting becomes very important indeed. They start prospecting once more, and then they build up the cash base again, build up the customers, get some more people in the pipeline. Then—alas!—they ease up again and relax, and they start taking it easy. Can you guess what happens a few months later?

That up-and-down cycle is purely a product of putting off the prospecting until the absolute last moment. And the cycle can be very dangerous. It can lead to the death of the business, actually. First-time entrepreneurs often underestimate the importance of keeping prospects in the pipeline at all times.

So prospecting—typically by making phone calls—has to be a daily activity. I've been quoted as saying that when God wanted to punish salespeople, He invented the cold call, and I think that is the case for entrepreneurs as well. Most of us don't particularly look forward to reaching out to new people, people we don't know, strangers, prospects, and talking to them about what we have to offer. But the secret of the whole process is that if you make a commitment to a very modest amount of work every day, you can have an incredibly positive effect on your income level and your business's future growth.

Whoever has this role of tracking down new business—and, as I've said, in my view it probably should be the president or the leader of the company—that person has to consistently make the calls on a day-in, day-out basis. You cannot leave prospecting for a week or two or three and hold off, and then come back to it again—unless you're very fond of roller-coaster rides.

In my own business, which has expanded to the point where we now have many salespeople, offices all over the country, and even international operations, I've always been loyal to my rule. I make ten cold calls every day that I'm not on the road or not giving a seminar. I will always—repeat, always—pick up the telephone and make ten prospecting calls before nine o'clock in the morning. And, by the way, that's a good strategy to use: Call early in the day. Sometimes you can reach some of the most important decision makers that way.

Ten calls for me is the magic number; that's my daily calling routine. You need to establish a calling routine that works for your industry, your situation. Why? Because significant increases in income are possible for you and your organization—if you make the most of the daily-call routine and follow up appropriately.

Let's assume that you pick up the phone and make fifteen

calls each and every day. In an average day, you speak to
seven decision makers and set up one new appointment. Over
the course of five business days, you'll have five new appointments each week—and perhaps three more appointments
that represent second or third visits. So you'll go out on something like eight appointments each week, and you'll close one
sale. That's a sale a week. Working fifty weeks out of the year,
your business will sign up fifty new sales.

But suppose you wanted to close a hundred new sales?
Suppose your income goals for the business made doubling
the revenue absolutely essential? How could you go about
doing that?

For beginning entrepreneurs who prospect by phone or
should be doing so (again, in my experience that's most of
them), the answer is pretty simple. In theory, there are only
five ways you could pull off the doubling trick:

1. *You could make twice as many calls during the course of
the day,* that is, make thirty rather than fifteen each and every
day. (It's possible, although some entrepreneurs will conclude that, given the time demands of the other elements of
the business, it's not a very realistic option.)

2. *You could get through to twice as many people,* that is,
speak to fourteen out of every fifteen people you dial. (That's
not very likely.)

3. *You could double the number of appointments you make
as the result of your phone work.* (Is it possible? Maybe.)

4. *You could double the number of sales you actually close
by improving your presentation and selling skills.* (Now, *that's*
a realistic possibility. I know, because I've trained lots and
lots of people who have ended up doing just that. But please
bear in mind, I'm not talking about using special "closing
tricks" to deliver twice as many customers. Instead, I'm talking about customizing your approach, asking the right questions, and listening carefully throughout the process—so that
a presentation is twice as likely to lead to a sale. I'll cover
interviewing, presentation, and closing in detail later on in
this book.)

5. *You could double the value of each sale by either raising your price or cross-selling more products or services.* That is to say, you can monetarily raise the value of the sale—or raise the value to the customer. (This is another realistic opportunity for significantly increasing sales income. By learning all you possibly can about the prospect, you'll increase the possibility that that person will be able to benefit from what your company has to offer. Again, that's part of interviewing, presentation, and closing.)

That's basically how the process works. By making calls every day, no matter what, and keeping track of the number of calls you make, you start to get an idea of how the "front" of the process—prospecting—affects the "back" of the process—the commitments you get from new customers.

The point to bear in mind, especially if you're new to the sales process, is that every rejection you get is essentially moving you closer to a sale. In other words, a rejection equals cash. *"No* means money" seems like a strange thing to say, but it's true.

When you're on the telephone with somebody who says that he has no interest whatsoever in talking to you about your office-cleaning services or the new widgets you have to offer, you've moved closer to your goal. By making that telephone call to someone who's in your target group, you've come closer to a sale. If you make twenty calls and clinch a single sale as a result of those calls, then each and every one of the calls that you connected on is worth cash to you—not just the call that finally culminated in the sale. Sales is a process, not an event, and it's a process that starts with prospecting.

It would be great if we lived in a world where everyone we spoke to automatically turned around and said, "Yes, that sounds like a great idea. Sign me up for a gross of the Model XJ Widgets," but we don't live in that world. We live in a world where sales happen, and that means that there are going to be some nos along with the yeses. In many cases, nineteen out of the twenty calls are going to result in a no.

And by the way, that *no* answer is "no for right now." I call those rejection calls fallback calls. To me there is no final *no*. There is always something to fall back on when you're looking for your next morning's calls. Keep track of the people who say *no*, and call them back one month or two months or three months later. You'll find that, in many cases, what they were really saying at the time was "Not right now. I'm not interested right now." Who knows what's going to be in play one month or two months or three months down the line. So don't even think about a *no* as a *no* per se. It's really a "no for now."

You're going to have to collect a fair number of those "no for now" in the course of your prospecting efforts to set up a single appointment that turns into a sale. And that's the objective of most cold calling, to set up an in-person appointment. You want to get together with your prospect, businessperson to businessperson, to talk about what you have to offer. Remember, since that appointment is with you, the entrepreneur, the person who started the business, the president of the company, your appeal carries a little bit more force, a little bit more drama, and a little bit more authority than it would if it came from "a salesperson."

What Does It Sound Like?

What follows is a very basic summary of some of the key points of your prospecting plan for your business. I go into greater detail on these issues in my book *The Consultant's Handbook*, published by Adams Media Corporation, and also in *High-Efficiency Selling*, which is available through John Wiley and Sons. For now, take a moment to get the "lay of the land" with this overview.

There are five big rules to follow when it comes to prospecting by phone.

RULE 1: **Schedule your day, your month, your quarter around prospecting.** It should be the very first thing you do in the morning, perhaps between eight and nine o'clock. Get on the telephone, track down new people, and ask for appointments. Eventually, you'll develop your own sense of how many calls you have to make to connect with a decision maker, how many of them you have to talk to in order to schedule an appointment, how many appointments you need to schedule to close a sale. Eventually, you'll learn to fine-tune your approach, working on each element of the process to maximize your income and hit your company's revenue goals. For now, just to get started, consider starting with fifteen cold calls every day, no matter what. Then track your numbers and see what they look like. Make a mental note that since you want to develop new cash sources for your business, prospecting must drive your day!

RULE 2: **Keep the script simple, and ask for appointments directly.** What exactly *do* you say to someone when you're making your prospecting calls? I'm going to give you a basic script and a basic turnaround strategy. These tools will help you through each and every one of those calls that you make. The following models work for literally hundreds of thousands of salespeople who have benefited from learning the DEI system. Try what is outlined here before you decide that the system is "not for me."

Some notes on terminology: A "suspect" is someone who has not yet made a commitment to move forward to a "next step" with you. When you call the ABC Company and you don't know the name of the president but are calling the president's office, that company and that president are "suspects." Once you have reached the president, had a conversation with him or her, and agreed to a clear next step, he or she has become a "prospect." The whole idea of "prospecting" is to turn "suspects" into "prospects"—to establish a mutually agreeable next step, typically an appointment. So that's what your script is meant to do. Here's what it might sound like:

Hello, Mr. Smith, this is John Jones from Power Sales here in Boston. I wanted to get in touch with you, Mr. Smith, to introduce you to our sales-training service, which was able to increase sales revenue for XYZ Company by forty percent in just one quarter. And I'm betting that your company, like XYZ, is interested in moving your sales revenue up to the next level. So, Mr. Smith, let's get together. How about Tuesday at ten o'clock in the morning?

RULE 3: **Don't reinvent the wheel!** Stick with the basic script outlined above. It's simple, it's direct, and it's been proven in hundreds of different business situations to work in turning suspects into prospects. Note that the script begins with the person's name, not with questions about how the contact is doing today, what the weather is like, whether or not the person watched the ball game, or anything else that doesn't relate to the question at hand. This script identifies you right off the bat, telling your name and the company you work for. It also gets you right to a recent success that you delivered for another customer. This should be something documentable, and if you're just getting started, it might be an initial assignment you took on, perhaps on a volunteer basis, or some sort of tangible result that you've been able to turn around or deliver to one of your customers or even to someone you're working with on a trial basis.

The script cuts right to the chase. It says, "Mr. Smith, let's get together." That again is the point of the prospecting call. You want to get face-to-face with the person. You must ask, without hesitation or apology, for the appointment, and you must propose a specific day and time. By doing so, you're taking action—you're asking the person to "play ball" with you. When you ask directly for an appointment, you are throwing the ball to the other person. You're going to do that dozens of times, to dozens of people. They can ignore the ball you've tossed, they can let it drop to the ground, they can catch it, they can bat it away, but they have to deal with it in some manner.

Your contact will become a prospect if he throws the ball back to you. If he says, "Well, gee, you know Tuesday's pretty busy for me, how about Thursday," then you've got an appointment. If he says, "You know what, we were interested in a sales-training setup like that, but we had our problems with it," then the ball's in your court again. If you get a dead-end no—"Absolutely not, we have no interest whatsoever"—then the person is not yet playing ball with you.

RULE 4: **Two and out!** What do you do when the person won't play ball? Make one more attempt during the call to turn around that objection, or at least to deal with it constructively.

Salespeople in general and entrepreneurs who are taking on this person-to-person salesperson role for the first time tend to get all bent out of shape over objections. They get intimidated by them—worked up over what exactly to say, how to respond, what psychological games to play to try to turn people around, to try to convince them that what they've said isn't accurate or valid. None of that works. All the tricks and fancy psychological maneuvers you read about in a lot of sales books simply don't work, so I'm not going to suggest that you use them.

What I'm going to suggest instead is an all-purpose objection response. This response will help you determine whether or not you're dealing with an honest-to-goodness roadblock, a "no for now" that's really stopping you in your tracks and is not going to let you move forward with this person today. It will also help you break through when you're dealing with someone who has a desk piled high with work and has a long to-do list, and who would really rather be attending to that than attending to you. And by the way, during your call, that's the main conflict you're going to have. The person would rather get back to what he or she was doing before than talk to you. What you're offering to discuss may not even register.

You're going to use a very simple turnaround technique, an all-purpose objection response, and if it doesn't work, you're going to move on to your next call. Rather than fighting with those people—rather than saying, "Well, why aren't you interested in getting the sort of results that we were able to put together with the XYZ Company?" or "Aren't you interested in saving money for your company?" or "How would your superior feel if he or she knew you were turning down the possibility to save money?" or any other invasive, crazy questions—try to introduce a new perspective. If the response that I suggest works, that's great; you'll try a second time to set up the appointment. If it doesn't, you're on to the next call. Remember, two tries for an appointment and out!

RULE 5: **Use the all-purpose turnaround.** Here's the response I want to suggest that you use for your turnaround. It's very basic and there are all kinds of variations, but as the foundation for your personal marketing program, I think you'll find it's incredibly efffective.

Think about the types of rejections you are likely to get when you try to get together to meet with someone to talk about what you have to offer. If you're like most entrepreneurs, you'll often hear people say things such as, "Well, we tried something like that before. It's too expensive." Or "We thought about that and the president thought it really didn't have a good match with our company." Or "We don't have the budget for that." Or "We do it a totally different way. We do that internally." Most sales situations feature three or four *very* common objections along these lines. When you hear them, you think to yourself, "Oh, that one again."

Are those sorts of responses really as hopeless as they sound? Have you ever sold to anyone who told you that initially? Perhaps when your contact had a chance to look at what you had to offer, it turned out that the budget wasn't quite as tight as he or she thought, or there was a way that the person could use the product or service to supplement what was going on internally. The truth is that the vast majority of the rejections entrepreneurs meet are ones that people eventually find a way to get past. So that's what you're going to say, honestly and directly.

Your turnaround response is based on the idea—which is true in the vast majority of selling environments and almost certainly true in yours—that most of the dead-end objections you hear are ones that you've heard before and have somehow managed to find a way to overcome. Ask yourself how you developed your first business relationship, or even implemented your first program at a previous job. Did you have to overcome skepticism that was similar to what you hear from prospects now? If you did, you can use this technique to your advantage. When your call results in a familar objection, you're simply going to say this:

> You know, Mr. Smith, that's what So-and So Company said to me before they had the chance to see how our training could supplement what they were already doing. In fact, because of a program we did for them a couple of months ago, they were able to track a twenty-two percent increase in sales as a result of the techniques we passed along in our sales training. So I really think, based on what you're saying here, that we ought to get together. How's Tuesday morning at ten o'clock?

That's your response. Now, you want to be very careful with this technique. You're not going to use this as a hammer to beat the prospect over the head to say, "You fool—you're not taking advantage of what So-and-So Company is doing." The tone is more conversational, more of a relaxed approach. (By the way, please remember that the script and turnaround texts I'm passing on are *rough* guidelines that are meant to be delivered in a natural tone—not rattled off as though you were an android.)

To recap, when making your second request for an appointment, you're going to say something along the following lines: "You know, it's interesting you mentioned that. I heard exactly the same type of comment from another company before they had a chance to find out what we offered them. I really think we ought to get together." And you're going to conclude with a specific date and time that you want to get together.

If, after those two attempts, you don't get a specific *yes* response or at least a midrange response ("You know what, Tuesday is not good. Can you call me back and we'll try for next week?"), you say, "Thank you very much," you hang up, and you move on to your next call. You do not want to engage in what we at DEI describe as gerbil selling.

What is gerbil selling? Have you ever seen a gerbil running around in those little wheels inside their cages? They go round and round and round and round and round and they don't ever move anywhere. Gerbil selling happens when you ask the prospect questions like:

> WHY don't you want to take advantage of what So-and-So Company used?
>
> DON'T you care about saving money?
>
> AREN'T you interested in delivering the best product to your customers?
>
> SHOULDN'T you be thinking about the best way to save on your life insurance expenses?

After the person has said "No, I'm not interested" twice, then it's time to get off the wheel and not go spinning around any more. Consider this suspect a fallback opportunity; call back in a month or two and try again. Remember, the secret in prospecting is moving on, collecting the nos when they're there, collecting the yeses when they're there, and delivering your message to a number of people consistently, day in and day out.

How People Will Respond to You

One final note about prospecting: The tone you take when you interact with someone on the phone has an enormous effect on the way that person responds to you.

People respond in kind. They will respond positively to positive input and negatively to negative input. So if you pick up your telephone and it's the end of the day and you're feeling grouchy, and you're bitter about some of the challenges you're facing, and you didn't sleep well the previous night, and you wish you were doing anything except calling up total strangers—that's not the best time to prospect! You want to make your calls when you radiate optimism, power, and authority; when you have a sense that if you connect up with a person, that's great, and that if you don't make a connection, there's somebody else to talk to on the next call. For me, that time is first thing in the morning.

I've been able to cover prospecting and objections in only a very cursory way in this chapter. For more detailed information on these important subjects, please see the books I've referenced or call DEI at 800-224-2140 for details about our publications and training programs.

Now that you know what the daily prospecting routine—the main tool you'll be using to "make something happen before lunch"—looks like, it's time to take a look at the other elements of the sales process. Remember, you're not asking for a *sale* during the prospecting phase, only for the opportunity to meet face-to-face with your contact. What happens next? How do prospects turn into customers? That's the subject of the next chapter.

27

THE SALES CYCLE

One of the most common errors first-time entrepreneurs make in their discussion with a new prospect is to assume that their company's competitors are their most important adversary. As a result, they spend a good deal of time talking to prospects about how much better they are than a certain company. Actually, the salesperson's most important opponent isn't Company X—it's the prospect's *current practices*.

After all, the prospect has a routine for handling the types of problems you can solve. His or her established set of habits is the first line of defense against any decision to change—not any individual company the prospect may or may not be working with at the moment.

The real competition you face is the status quo, what's going on right now. Let's face it. Prospects don't sit around waiting for someone to call about a possible change in their long-distance service. Instead, they probably think, "What's the problem with what I've got? Where's the crisis? Why should I change? Don't I have enough problems to solve already without changing something that doesn't need changing?" If they "needed" a change, they would have called someone already!

You may have something of value to offer, but you can't start lecturing the prospect about it at the beginning of the relationship, because he or she is focused on something that's already working—or, at least, appears to be working

Now, you can sell by completely ignoring how the prospect feels about the status quo. You just won't sell as much as you could. At DEI, we like to say that of all the sales you could possibly close, one-third are going to come your way just for showing up at the right time; one-third aren't going to go your way, regardless of what you do; and one-third will go your way once you master the sales cycle. That means you will do best once you accept that at the outset of your relationship with the prospect, he or she already has something that works at some level. Even prospects who "hate their current vendors," but have taken no action to find another one, must be approached with an open mind.

So the first point to remember is this: What's taking place in the present makes sense to the prospect. That means that making a suggestion at the very beginning of the relationship that he or she change what currently makes sense probably isn't the best way to maximize any given sales rep's income.

If you walked into a prospect's office and noticed that there was a large, brown cow in front of his or her desk, munching away at the carpet, what would you do? I can tell you one thing, your best course of action *wouldn't* be to start talking about how much more healthful the milk your company offers is than the milk your prospect is enjoying right now. Why not? Why shouldn't you pull out that one-size-fits-all brochure and simply read it verbatim to your potential customer? Because you don't know enough about this person yet!

For all you know, the reason that cow is in the office is that the person behind the desk enjoys the "moo" sound it makes.

Maybe your contact is lactose-intolerant but enjoys the company of cows! You don't know! So you have to ask. You have to ask questions like, "Why did you choose to put a cow in the office? How did you go about deciding this was the right cow for you? How did you get this particular cow?"

That's very different from the way most people sell. Most people take a glance at the cow, nod briskly, and start launching into a memorized sales pitch about how much vitamin D their milk offers. That's not the best way to build relationships! The only thing you know for sure as you walk in that door is that *keeping a cow in the office makes sense to this person.* Beyond that, you've got to ask questions, take careful notes, and do what you can to keep the person engaged and "playing ball" with you. Let's look in a little more detail at what this "ball-playing" process looks like—and at what its competition looks like.

Beyond ABC

There's a philosophy in the sales world known as ABC—Always Be Closing—that leads to a very common selling model. Some sales managers swear by the ABC method. I'm not one of them.

ABC is the school of thought that advises salespeople, in essence, to assume that all the potential customers they encounter are more or less identical. Therefore, you should ask for the business from the minute you encounter someone who sounds as if he or she could conceivably be your customer.

Many ABC adherents will challenge me on this, say that I'm oversimplifying, that I've left out all kinds of initial bonding steps that ABC selling encourages. If I'm exaggerating, it's not by much. Anyone who's ever received a call from a telemarketer who tries to close before you have the chance to contribute anything meaningful to the conversation can attest to that.

"How old are the windows in your home, sir?"

"They're not my windows—I rent an apartment."

"Okay, but if you did own the home, sir, how old would the windows be? Wouldn't you like to learn how to cut down on those heating bills you'd be paying if you did actually own the house?"

To my way of thinking, the ABC method is an amazingly ineffective way to sell. Think about how it operates. Someone sits down with a prospect, asks an impersonal "warm-up question" or two, like "Are you the person I should be talking to?" and (surprise, surprise) gets little or no important information as a result.

The problem with asking "Are you the person I should be talking to?" or any other questions like it is that prospects rarely, if ever, volunteer their unimportance to us. The temptation is always there for the prospect to answer that question with less than completely accurate information—whether the intention is to cover for a busy boss, or to learn more about our service, or to be able to deliver a quick *no* and get back to that to-do list. ABC salespeople assume—erroneously—that they will get meaningful answers at the very outset of the relationship with the prospect. In fact, as any experienced salesperson will attest, the quality of the information one receives from a brand-new prospect starts out as rather suspect and improves dramatically as you develop your relationship with the contact.

After a few of these "probing questions," the ABC salesperson determines—or at least appears to determine—that the company is using, say, a pocket pager. So what does the ABC system suggest the salesperson do? Always Be Closing, right?

"Pocket pagers? We have pocket pagers! We've got a plan that's just right for you!"—which is pretty amazing, since the rep knows nothing about how the prospect uses the pagers!

There follows a brief summary of all the wonderful things that the salesperson's pocket pager can do for the prospect. At DEI, we call this phase the product dump because it's a context-free recitation of information, much of it totally irrelevant to the prospect. But that doesn't stop countless sales reps—maybe even some of yours—from attempting to make a full presentation right then and there. They do it by means of what I call a slapshot response. They respond instantly, and without enough information, to a prospect—and then try to close. If the unwitting prospect is unfortunate enough to mention that she uses pagers, or an 800-number service, or PHONECO long-distance service—then *smack!* the rep has a response: "We can beat PHONECO!" *Slapshot!*

Can your reps beat PHONECO? Sure they can! But in a world where communications customers are buffeted regularly with competing claims from competing phone companies, wouldn't it make sense to find out a little bit about how the customer is using the system you want to replace? After all, what's the alternative?

> "Gee, I notice there's a big cow in the middle of your office. Was that your idea?"
>
> "Yep. I had that cow shipped in here about three months ago."
>
> "Hey, that's great. You know, our cow gives more milk than the cow you've currently got in your office!" *Slapshot!*

What if I hate drinking milk? What if my cow is there to relax me? Or to serve as a conversation piece? Or to impress an important client who visits me regularly and has a mania for taking pictures of cows? All that talk about milk won't make any difference to me!

The slapshot selling model looks like this:

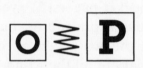

The *O* stands for "Opening," the *P* stands for "Present," and the *C* stands for "Close." Notice how big that *C* is. ABC sales reps spend a huge amount of their time trying to close sales in the slapshot model. They introduce themselves, they bat a few questions around, and then they try to Always Be Closing.

As abrasive as it is, and as uncomfortable as it makes the vast majority of prospects who encounter it, the slapshot model will result in sales sometimes. (Remember what I said earlier about how one-third of the sales happen because people show up at the right time?) But the slapshot model won't deliver as many sales as your reps deserve.

Now take a look at the DEI model of the sales cycle:

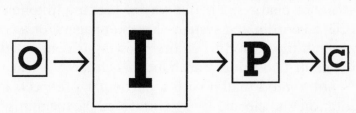

The cycle has four phases: *O*pening (which corresponds to the prospecting or cold-calling work we discussed in the last chapter), *I*nterviewing, *P*resentation, and *C*losing. Notice that the smallest element here is the close—and the largest element is the interview. In fact, the interview should constitute three-quarters of the time you spend with a contact whom you want to turn into a customer. The close, if you manage the sale properly, should be a tiny point at the far right-hand corner of the process.

The objective of each phase in the model sales cycle is to move ahead to the next phase. When you're prospecting, the objective is to get the prospect to agree to move forward into a meaningful interview phase by agreeing to a face-to-face meeting. When prospects are in the interview phase, the objective is to get the prospect to help you track down the information necessary to develop a presentation that fits the prospect like a glove. When they're in the presentation phase, the objective is to conduct it so well that the prospect agrees to become a customer when we say, "It makes sense to me— what do you think?" (That's the best "closing technique" I can offer you.)

Interviewing enables you to find out exactly what's important to the prospect. If a price analysis of phone service is in order, the interviewing phase is where you get all the relevant information, make a realistic estimate of the amount of time necessary to complete that analysis, and offer a one-professional-to-another prediction of what's likely to result from that analysis. (It could sound something like this: "Let me tell you what we usually find out that we can do for customers in your industry . . .") The interviewing phase is where you learn whether a prospect is looking for a ten percent reduction in long-distance charges, a better way of keeping in touch with the CEO, a coordinated system of pocket pagers, or a combination of all three. And when interviewing is conducted correctly, one of two things can happen—either you learn that there's not a good match with a particular prospect, or the presentation and closing lead to informed partnerships.

Remember, the point of the sales cycle is to get the prospect to "play ball" with you, to move the process forward one stage at a time. If the prospect is playing ball, you will be developing a portfolio of information that will make the presentation and eventually the close possible. If the prospect isn't playing ball, you need to stop investing time in this relationship and find someone else to call.

That's the sales cycle in a nutshell. Most people make the mistake of assuming that closing the sale is what creates revenue. Closing is only a confirmation. What actually creates the revenue is *prospecting*.

The next chapter goes into more detail about how to manage the prospects you'll be working with. After all, they're driving the whole process! You'll find out how to create an essential tool—your prospect board—to keep your prospects for future revenue strong in both the short and long terms. In the chapters that follow that one, you'll learn how to make the other three phases of the sales cycle, interviewing, presentation, and closing—the ones that follow your cold calling/prospecting work—fall into place, too.

28

PROSPECT MANAGEMENT IS BUSINESS MANAGEMENT

The prospect-management system I'm about to outline for you is not complex. If you follow these instructions and maintain your base of prospects as I suggest, you will even out your company's revenue performance and be able to maintain it at a high level that is consistent and makes sense for your organization.

No more dramatic ups and downs. No more blood-pressure-raising peaks and valleys. There will be variations in your totals from week to week and month to month, of course, but they won't be overwhelming variations. The changes you see won't be part of one of those energy-consuming, boom-and-bust cycles so many salespeople fall prey to. They'll be variations that fall within the outlines of a plan—your company's plan.

If you use this prospect-management system, you'll be able to assume full control of your sales routine, predict your income—and make the end-of-the-year crunch a distant memory. Maintaining your prospect base effectively is the key to developing a constant revenue stream for your business.

The Prospect Board

Take a look now at the prospect board. It's the nerve center of your prospect-management system. You'll see that it's broken down into six columns. From left to right, they are:

- Fallback/Opportunity
- First Appointment
- Twenty-five percent probability
- Fifty percent probability
- Ninety percent probability
- Closed

What do these columns represent? Many salespeople, when they first look at the columns on the board, think each col-

EXHIBIT 6

Prospect-Management Board Criteria

FB/O	FA	1/25	1/50	1/90	C
OPPORTUNITY	*DATE	GOOD FA	FINAL PROPOSAL PRESENTED	CONTRACT AWAITING SIGNATURE	SIGNED CONTRACT
SUSPECT	*TIME	INFORMATION GATHERING BEGUN/IN PROCESS			
CANDIDATE			*RIGHT PERSON	VERBAL AGREEMENT	
LEAD					
REFERRAL			*REAL $		
			*REAL TIMETABLE		
"FALL BACK" (prospect that didn't close)	SCHEDULED FIRST MEETING	SCHEDULED NEXT STEP	SCHEDULED NEXT STEP	SCHEDULED NEXT STEP	
		*25% likely	*50% likely	*90% likely	
		←———————— PROSPECTS ————————→			
	1–2 WEEKS	1–2 WEEKS	1–2 WEEKS	1–2 WEEKS	

The Sales Cycle

1 DAY ————————	4 WEEKS ————————	→ 8 WEEKS
MINIMUM	AVERAGE	MAXIMUM

umn must represent a predetermined period of time—a month or week of the year, say. Actually, each column represents a category of probability of sale.

The column on the far left-hand side of the board features contacts that have the least probability of turning into sales (typically, people you haven't called yet or people who have expressed only a minimal interest in what you have to offer). The column on the far right-hand side of the board features contacts that have just turned into sales. The four columns in the middle track everything else.

Take a moment now to pull out your own list of potential prospects. You're going to take a look at your real-life prospect base, and you're going to start assigning each prospect to one of the six categories on the board and make cards for them. Before you do, though, please remember this simple principle, the idea that guides everything you do with the prospect-management system: Your aim is always to transfer cards to the next highest category.

If a card is in the fallback/opportunity column, your goal is to set a first appointment. If you set a first appointment, your goal is to move the card into the twenty-five percent category. If you succeed in doing that, your goal is to move the card into the fifty percent category. If the card progresses to fifty percent, your goal is to get it into ninety percent. If the card makes it into ninety percent, your goal is to close the sale.

Winning business for your firm is a dynamic job, one in which situations change from day to day (or even moment to moment!). So the cards should always move. And you should focus your efforts on getting them to move from left to right.

THE LEFT-HAND COLUMNS

The first column, as we've seen, is for opportunities. It's for people who may be the source of a sale at some point, but who don't at the moment represent revenue we should count on. These are unqualified leads, people you have little or no information about, or people who have said *no* to your product or service in the past but whom you wish to keep on your target list. As I've mentioned, they may turn into business in the future!

This opportunities column is for people whom you want to see but who aren't sure they want to see you yet. It's the "softest" of all the columns on the board.

The second column, the first-appointment group, represents people who have agreed to meet with you at some point in the future. You haven't met with them yet. You've scheduled an appointment. Whether that appointment is set for two weeks from now or tomorrow afternoon, this is someone with whom you have an agreement to meet, someone whom you haven't yet met to discuss your product or service.

Those two are pretty simple, right? Take a moment now to set up cards for people in your prospect base who fall into these two categories. Specify the contact name, if you have it, and the name of the organization.

THE TWENTY-FIVE PERCENT COLUMN

This third column is reserved for contacts who have a twenty-five percent probability of turning into sales. How do you know whether the person represents a twenty-five percent chance of turning into business for you? Simple. If you've already met with a prospect and if that prospect has agreed to meet with you a second time or you strongly anticipate that a second meeting with the prospect will be forthcoming, then it's reasonable to assume that the organization in question represents a one in four chance of turning into a sale.

If you've met with the person, but he or she hedges about the second meeting or rejects the idea entirely, then guess what? That prospect shouldn't go into the twenty-five percent column. That organization may represent an opportunity for income sometime in the future, but there's not a realistic chance of closing a sale right now.

If, on the other hand, you've had your first meeting, and

the prospect agrees to your request to set up a second meeting, that card should go into the twenty-five percent column.

In other words, if you've had your first meeting and you receive unmistakable signals that the prospect is still interested in playing ball with you, that prospect's card goes into the twenty-five percent column.

If you can, consider your own best prospects right now—the people who represent your best bets for business over the next few months. (If you haven't yet done any prospecting work for your business, that's all right, but remember, the sooner you can complete the following exercises with real, live leads, the better off your revenue totals are going to look.)

Set up individual cards for those people who have met with you initially and who are interested in your product. Do the same for the people who have agreed to a second appointment. Do the same for the people who want to talk about what you have to offer but about whom you don't yet know enough to make a formal proposal. Those people belong in your twenty-five percent column. Write the name of the organization and the name of the contact on each card, and place the cards in the twenty-five percent column.

THE FIFTY PERCENT COLUMN

So, you have a meeting or two. You gather some information. You develop a proposal. You work on conducting the interview phase perfectly (using the questioning techniques you'll be reading about in later chapters). You make your presentation. You show your prospect what it is that you're proposing. After that presentation, the prospect is still interested in talking with you about what you have to offer. Perhaps the prospect has agreed to discuss in much greater detail than before the specifics of what your organization has to offer. All of this means that you probably now have at least a fifty percent chance of closing this sale. You've made a presentation, and the prospect is still interested in playing ball.

Our definition of a presentation is simple. You'll know

you've entered the presentation phase—the fifty percent phase—because you'll be discussing real dollars and a real timetable. At this point, you have a legitimate expectation of closing the sale in one out of two cases.

Believe me, it won't take long for you to know when someone is interested in talking in detail about what you have to offer—and when someone isn't. As an entrepreneur, you'll also know that there's not much to be gained by deluding yourself into believing that this kind of conversation is taking place when it's not.

So, are you having that kind of talk with your prospect? This fifty percent column asks you to give your best, most realistic answer to the following questions:

- Is this person clearly a decision maker?
- Is this person willing to discuss timetables and dollar figures with me?
- Is this person willing to commit the time and energy required to discuss my company's product or service during another in-person meeting?

If the answer to any of these questions is *no*, you should not move a card from the twenty-five percent column to the fifty percent column. Instead, you should leave it where it is, move it back into the opportunity column, or remove it from the board altogether.

If a card is occupying a spot in the fifty percent column, that means (1) you're talking with the right person about the specifics of your product or service, and (2) that person is willing or highly likely to make a clear time commitment to you to discuss precisely what you have to offer. A prospect who is unwilling to schedule a future appointment with you or discuss timetables should not be in the fifty percent category.

Take a moment now to review your own prospects. Set up cards, with the name of the organization and the name of your contact, for all the prospects that you believe should fall into the fifty percent category. Put them in the fifty percent column on your board.

Be honest! Be realistic! Be fair to yourself! Don't assign cards to the fifty percent level that don't belong there!

THE NINETY PERCENT COLUMN

Cards that go in the ninety percent column represent prospects who are all but sold. This is the closest you can get to closing the sale without a signed contract in your hand.

Lots of salespeople fall into the trap of saying something has a ninety percent chance of closing when it really doesn't. The question here isn't how excited you are about the prospect, but how excited the prospect is about doing business with you.

At my company, we like to say that the ninety percent column is exclusively for prospects that can be considered COD. That stands for "contract on desk." If the person you're talking to has your organization's contract on his or her desk and you have a very strong expectation that the sale will close, the card should be in the ninety percent column. If there's genuine interest on the prospect's part but there is no contract on the desk and you do not have a realistic expectation that the sale will close, the card should not be in the ninety percent column. In all likelihood, it still belongs in the fifty percent column.

Remember, nine out of ten of the cards you place in this column should result in honest-to-goodness business for you and your organization. You've presented your proposal, you've set up the contract, and you expect to have that contract back in a week or two. Take a moment now to place all of your current prospects who fall into this category into the ninety percent column on your board.

A QUIZ

Suppose you have the card "ABC Widget Company" in your opportunity column. You call up ABC Widget, find out that Joe McEvoy is in charge of making decisions regarding your product or service, and reach Joe directly. Answer the question following each of these seven scenarios about what might happen after you call this company.

1. You ask Joe to set up an appointment with you, but he refuses. Where should the card for ABC Widget go?

2. You ask Joe to set up an appointment with you, and he agrees. You are scheduled to meet tomorrow morning at eight o'clock. Where should the card for ABC Widget go?

3. You ask Joe to set up an appointment with you, and he agrees. You are scheduled to meet three weeks from now. Where should the card for ABC Widget go?

4. You ask Joe to set up an appointment with you. He agrees, and you get together, but the meeting doesn't seem to go very well. At the conclusion of this meeting, you ask Joe to set a second appointment with you. He makes some excuse about how busy he is this week, says that he may be able to work something out after things calm down a bit, then concludes the meeting. Where should the card for ABC Widget go?

5. You ask Joe to set up an appointment with you. He agrees, you get together, and the meeting goes very nicely. At the conclusion of this meeting, you ask Joe to set a second appointment with you to discuss in more detail his objectives and how you may be able to help him meet them. He agrees. Where should the card for ABC Widget go?

6. You ask Joe to set up an appointment with you. He agrees, and you get together, and this meeting goes superbly. You set an appointment for a second meeting, and at that meeting you discuss your price list and the dates your product could actually be delivered. Joe seems very interested as the meeting draws to a close and schedules a meet-

ing with you to discuss a few more details with some of the senior people at ABC Widget.

Where should the card for ABC Widget go?

7. You ask Joe to set up an appointment with you. He agrees, and you get together, and the meeting seems promising. At the conclusion of this meeting, you ask Joe to set a second appointment with you. He does. Halfway through that second meeting, he calls in some of the senior people at ABC, which you didn't expect. The other people listen to what you have to say and ask about delivery dates. They like what they're hearing. As the meeting closes, you suggest that you have your people draw up a contract based on the points that have been discussed at that day's meeting. Joe and his associates agree. Everyone is all smiles. That afternoon, you set up the contract and mail it out.

Where should the card for ABC Widget go?

ANSWERS: (1) back in the opportunity column—or, if you prefer, off the board completely; (2) in the first-appointment column; (3) in the first-appointment column; (4) back in the opportunity column—or, if you prefer, off the board completely; (5) in the twenty-five percent column; (6) in the fifty percent column; (7) in the ninety percent column.

Some Common Questions About the Prospect-Management System

1. Are all of my unqualified leads supposed to go in the opportunity column?

Probably not. If you included them all, your opportunity column could be many times the length of the column space we've shown. We find that salespeople are usually most comfortable working with ten or so opportunities at any given time.

2. I've got a prospect that doesn't seem to fall into any of the categories you've described! What should I do?

This shouldn't happen very often, but if it does, don't despair. Occasionally, you'll run into an organization that doesn't seem to match up with anything on the board—for example, a situation where there are dual-decision makers, one of whom is ecstatic about what you have to offer, and the other of whom can't stand the sight of you—but those situations should be pretty rare.

Put the "exception" card aside and deal with it individually. Don't use it as an excuse not to keep the rest of the cards on the board up-to-date.

Beware of the "prospect" who isn't really a prospect. Let's say you met with the people at XYZ Systems three weeks ago. They wouldn't give you a second appointment, but they said they were "very interested" in what you have to offer.

That's what they said. You've called them twice a week for the last three weeks. They won't commit to another meeting with you. Now you have to ask yourself, How interested are these people?

If you have no appointment and no realistic likelihood of an appointment, then you have no prospect. No matter how well the conversation goes, no matter how pleasant your contact is, this organization does not represent imminent business to you. Put the card in the opportunity category, or take it off the board.

The same advice goes for your dealings with the people at Acme Supply Company, who were enthralled by the detailed in-person presentation you gave during your third meeting with them six weeks ago. Today, however, they won't take your call. Get them off the active part of the board!

3. What else do I need to put on the card besides the name of my contact and the name of the organization?

You need to specify what's going to happen next—and when! Cards that make it out of the opportunity category should be updated regularly. Date the cards.

Remember, we're talking about a dynamic system. A card that stays in the same place for any significant length of time probably reflects a problem. If you notice after two or three weeks, perhaps, that a card hasn't been going anywhere, you should either put it back in the opportunity column or take it out of the system.

All of the cards that make it out of the opportunity category should have a clear next step—either a call you plan to make or a meeting you have arranged with the prospect—detailed on the card. If you cannot answer the question "When am I going to see this person next?" there is a very strong possibility that you are not dealing with an active prospect. This person may belong in the opportunity category or may need to be taken off the board.

What the Board Should Look Like

Because first appointments drive the entire process, and because unproductive leads are constantly being weeded out of the system, a board that is set up intelligently for the long term has a very specific look.

In the opportunity column you should probably have ten or so cards representing people with whom you want to schedule appointments. The precise number of cards in this column actually isn't all that important, because it's not really an active column, which the rest of the columns are.

In the first-appointment column you should, ideally, have the most cards of any active group. These are cards that represent the people who are driving the whole process: prospects you have not met with before, but who have agreed to sit down with you and discuss what you have to offer.

In the twenty-five percent column you should have somewhat fewer cards than in the first-appointments column.

In the fifty percent column you should have somewhat fewer cards than in the twenty-five percent column.

In the ninety percent column you should have fewer cards still.

In the final column, which reflects recently closed sales, you should have a still smaller number of cards.

What the Board Shouldn't Look Like

If your ninety percent column has four times as many cards in it as your twenty-five percent column, what does that say? Well, it probably says that you've got some unrealistic expectations about the business you'll be closing in the near future.

A good many salespeople overestimate the likelihood of closing the cards they put in the ninety percent category. Don't fall into that trap. Around my office, we keep a very close eye on cards that get placed in the ninety percent column. If over the course of two or three weeks, nine out of ten of these cards don't turn into revenue, we try to figure out why people are miscategorizing their leads, and we try to help them look at things more realistically.

If you're confident of the accuracy of the categories you've assigned your cards to and you find that the first-appointment category is shorter than it ought to be, there's another problem to work on. When you've got almost everything in the fifty percent column and very little in the way of initial appointments, you're shortchanging yourself! If it takes you, say, five weeks to close a sale, then five weeks from today that fifty percent column will be empty, and you'll be wondering why the bottom has dropped out of your revenue. The answer? You weren't focusing on prospecting today.

If you don't set up first appointments now, you won't have anything showing up in the other columns later on, and you'll hit a "sales valley"!

First appointments drive the prospect-management system. If your board doesn't show that the first-appointment column is the longest active column on the board, you need to do more prospecting—or get ready for an income vacuum later on in the process!

Dates Count!

Update your board regularly. I recommend reviewing and appropriately updating the cards every business day. And please remember that you can tell how serious someone is by how detailed the dates are that they pass along.

Someone who tells you he's interested in meeting with you "sometime next month" is not as strong a prospect as the person who agrees to meet with you "this coming Tuesday at two-thirty."

Someone who says she wants to consider a seminar program "in the near future" is not as strong a prospect as someone who says she's interested in discussing a program for "the second and third weeks of next month, when all the customer-service people in the northeast region will be scheduled for training."

This system allows you to identify prospects' quality very quickly and very accurately. If you have a specific date on a card for a mutually agreed upon next step with this prospect, that's good news; that means you may stand a good chance of being able to advance that particular card to the next stage.

If you don't have a date, you may not want to focus quite as much effort on that card!

What Are You Trying to Accomplish?

Do you know what your prospect is doing? When you meet with your contact, do you have a sense of the problems he or she is trying to overcome, the main objective he or she is hoping to attain? Do you know what it is about your product or service that will help this prospect accomplish that objective? If the answer to any of these questions is *no*, you're going to have a hard time building a meaningful business relationship with the prospect.

Your objective is always to move the cards ahead to the next column and, ultimately, to the close. You can't do that without knowing how you'll be helping the prospect to accomplish the important goals he or she has defined.

You must know what the prospect hopes to get accomplished, not what you think he or she needs. And you must know what you plan to do at the next meeting that will highlight your ability to help turn the prospect's objective into a reality. Are you gathering more information about the objective? Developing a program that targets the objective—and encouraging the prospect's input? Making a formal presentation based on what you've learned from the prospect?

You Can't Cheat!

The prospect board is a tool. The more accurate the information you feed into it, the more accurate the information you will get from it.

If you overestimate the likelihood of a particular lead turning into dollars, you'll only be fooling yourself. And believe me, it won't take long for you to find out that the information you fed into the system wasn't realistic! If you set up a board and fill it with prospects who aren't willing to talk seriously about doing business with you, you'll be in for a very rude awakening a few weeks down the line.

Anticipating Revenue

What does the future hold for you in terms of income? The (approximate) answer is probably easier to learn than you think. If you're eager to find out about the income you're likely to receive from the prospects you're currently tracking on the board, read on.

Assign a value (say, your likely revenue that would be generated) to all the cards in your twenty-five percent, fifty percent, and ninety percent columns. Add up all the figures in the twenty-five percent column; then multiply to determine twenty-five percent of that figure. Add up all the figures in the fifty percent column; then divide that in half. Add up all the figures in the ninety percent column; then subtract ten percent of the total. Add these amounts together, and you'll have a pretty good idea of what the revenue arising from your total current prospect base will be.

How Do You Feel About What Your Board Looks Like?

Many entrepreneurs perform the exercise we've been doing—assigning categories to all their current prospects—and are a little uncomfortable about what their board shows. Sometimes, estimating the revenue from their current prospect base makes them feel a little uneasy.

That's good! The whole point of the system is to show you what you need to work on right now. It's better to know about a problem and be in a position to do something about it, than it is to have no idea that the problem exists.

If you're looking at your board, and you notice that you don't have enough cards in the twenty-five percent category, then you probably already know what you need to do! Schedule more first appointments so you can get some people agreeing to second appointments!

At the risk of repeating myself, I want to remind you of the single most important point associated with this system: The front end is what makes the whole process work. Don't get distracted by "sure thing" prospects who won't commit to anything and neglect your first-appointments column!

Ask yourself, Are there enough new leads, new first appointments, to generate next week's (or next month's or next quarter's) fifty percent column? The fact that you have twenty "great conversations" a week is less important than the fact that you need sixteen first-time appointments scheduled over the coming two weeks in order to hit a particular income goal.

Suppose you find that an uncomfortably large number of your prospects aren't following through after you give a proposal? If your proposals aren't leading to closes, there's a very good chance that you're not getting enough information early on in the process. Think about ways you can refine your first-interview approach. Are you asking the right questions? Are you asking any questions? Are you listening to the prospect—or are you simply reading the contents of your brochure to your contact person?

You Can Take Control!

Selling does not have to be difficult for the entrepreneur—unless you make it difficult by letting the selling process slip out of your control. The prospect-management system allows you to assume personal control of your face-to-face marketing efforts and to evaluate exactly where you are at any moment. If you use it each and every day, you'll know how your prospecting efforts will eventually pay off for your business, and you'll also have a tangible reminder of where you stand with each individual lead in your prospect base.

When you come back from a sales call, you'll have to look at the board and decide whether or not you should advance the card from the first-appointment column to the twenty-five percent column. If you have a card in column five that you feel is going to close, but three or four weeks pass and it doesn't close, then you'll have to reevaluate how much effort you should commit to that account.

Never forget, appointments drive the process! The first appointment leads to the first meeting. The first meeting leads to the second meeting. The second meeting leads to the presentation and/or the third meeting. The presentation leads to the close. Cards will drop out at each stage of the process, but every one of your sales will go through a cycle that is similar to this. And the more first appointments you set, the more candidates for revenue you have on the board.

By looking at the dates on the board, you can see very quickly whether or not a particular lead is taking significantly longer to move forward than the average sale you close. The more a lead exceeds that average amount of time, the less likely you are to get revenue from it.

This is an extremely important point. If it takes you ninety days to close your average sale, you'll know when the odds have started to turn against your ever getting revenue out of a given lead. When a prospect has been on the board more than ninety days, you can rest assured that the odds of the sale closing have gone down significantly.

By using this prospect-management system, you'll gain deeper insight into your own typical sales cycle. You'll learn where you're having difficulty and get a pretty clear idea about what you should be doing to correct things. And you'll be continually reminded of one of the main jobs you face as an entrepreneur who's also serving as a salesperson—keeping the appointments coming and moving as many prospects as you can along to the next stage.

Now it's time to look in depth at the interviewing phase of your sales cycle.

29

ONE ON ONE

Earlier I made reference to an important part of the sales cycle that all too many entrepreneurs overlook entirely: the interview.

The ability to ask the right questions during interviews with prospects is one of the most important skills you can develop. That's what we're going to be focusing on in this chapter.

At DEI we define selling as: asking people what they do, how they do it, where they do it, who they do it with, why they do it that way—and then finding out how we can help them do it better.

That's selling in a nutshell. Our experience, though, is that most salespeople—and most beginning entrepreneurs who engage in face-to-face selling—don't ask the kinds of questions that make this question-based selling possible. They're eager to "find a match" as quickly as possible, so they assume that all prospects are identical. Managing the interview process effectively means making sure that you don't make this mistake. Be prepared to shake hands, admire the surroundings, and give a *brief* summary of your business and history at the beginning of your meeting with the prospect. You should have a client list or summary of references with you; if your prospect asks for it at the outset of your meeting, pass it along, but otherwise wait until the end of your session to discuss what you've done for others. Then, after the preliminaries, instead of launching into a preprogrammed monologue or pulling out your brochure, pull out a pad of paper and a pen. Look the prospect in the eye and write down the answers you receive to key questions.

Don't trust your memory! Write down everything you hear—good, bad, and indifferent. This provides you with an essential record of the meeting—and it also encourages your prospect to open up to you. And let's face it, having someone write down your every spoken word is pretty flattering.

What should you ask? Here are some examples:

What do you do here? or *What's the main thing you're trying to accomplish in such-and-such an area?* (Have you hooked up with a talent agency, an executive-recruiting firm, a manufacturing concern, a printing company, a construction company? Each of these operations will use your products and services in a very different way.)

How do you do that? (What activities does the company or department perform to accomplish its goals?)

Where do you do that? (Are there other offices? Does the organization conduct its business in this particular area? Throughout the state? Throughout the region? Nationally? Internationally?)

Why do you do it that way? (One classic form for this question sounds like this: "That's interesting. I'm just curious— why did you decide to do that?")

How can we help you do that better? (This is not the same as asking, "Don't you want to save money by using our widget-cleaning service?")

A story we tell at DEI shows how that final question can develop naturally from the rest. A museum was unable to get its insurance for precious works of art to kick in during a critical period of time—the period after paintings on loan had arrived at the museum's central facility but before the assessor could inspect and catalog them. A sales rep for an instant-camera company made a multiple-unit sale to the facility, but she didn't do it by asking, "Why don't you use instant cameras in your operations?" Nobody at the museum had thought about using instant cameras, so she wouldn't have gotten a constructive response by asking a question like that. She found out, during an interview, about a particular decision maker's particular objective—make those dangerous three-to-four-day lags between arrival and insurance coverage go away. Then, after thoughtful, open-minded discussions with her contact, she made a proposal: "Based on what you've told me here today, it sounds like you might be able to use a couple of our instant cameras to catalog your recent arrivals. You could overnight the photos and logs to your insurance carrier, save their representative a trip, and get your coverage in place within forty-eight hours. That's what a lot of the other museums we've worked with have found makes sense."

It worked! But it wouldn't have if the rep hadn't found out what the museum did before launching into a preprogrammed "spiel." The same goes for your sales meetings with prospects. The more you find out about each and every area of a prospect's business that has some possible connection to what you offer, the more able you are to find a possibility for a business relationship.

Once again, the key questions are:

- What does the person do?
- How does he or she do it?
- Where does he or she do it?
- Why does he or she do it that way?
- How can you help him or her do it better?

The Slapshot, Again

Superior selling results arise from partnerships. Partnerships come about, not because salespeople use tricks to get people to buy, but because salespeople know how to listen and are open to finding ways to match up what they have to offer with what the prospect . . .

Time out. How would you finish that sentence?

With "needs"?

Remember, the status quo is what you are really competing against. If the prospect "needed" a different widget-cleaning service, he or she would have gone out and arranged for it already. "Need" means you can't do without something!

Effective selling is based on listening during that all-important interview phase to determine what the prospect . . . is trying to get accomplished. That's very different from what the prospect "needs," and it's usually different from prospect to prospect.

You want to present a plan that makes sense to the prospect. Too many entrepreneurs get caught up in the trap of believing that there's some magic involved in that final closing phase, some special incantation they can say that will turn unwilling prospects into customers, even though the prospects haven't been encouraged to reveal anything meaningful about themselves. It doesn't work that way!

When I say "It doesn't work that way," I mean that slapshot selling is not the way to get superior results for your organization—that one-third of possible sales we talked about earlier that depends on your skills. Slapshot selling does result in customers . . . sometimes. But what about the depth of sale? What about the dollar value of the sale? What about the possibility of closing a sale that, now or later, results in multiple applications of your product or service? What about developing a relationship with a customer who will stick with you when a competitor calls or at least give you the chance to match what the competition offers? All of these depend on interview-based selling—not slapshot selling, in which the salesperson instantly says things like: "We have widget-cleaning services, too!" "We offer eight hundred lines, too!" "We have affordable service contracts, too!" These immediate responses stand in the way of good interviewing, which should ideally occupy around seventy-five percent of your reps' sales cycle with any given prospect. (Remember how big that *I* for "Interviewing" looks in the ideal sales model?)

If you find yourself rocketing forward to your presentation without any real sense of the individual prospect's current (and unique!) situation, the odds are that you're shortchanging yourself by skipping or abbreviating the interview phase of the sales cycle.

Interviewing Is the Center of the Sales Process

It is important to remember that effective interviewing

- takes time
- encourages correction, because when we allow the prospect to correct us, everybody wins
- is not product-focused (that is, doesn't use statements such as "Well, we have that, too!")
- doesn't immediately jump to the presentation
- builds around the question—whether it's stated directly or contained within another question—"What are you trying to accomplish?"
- occupies about seventy-five percent of the successful sales cycle
- helps you identify prospects you shouldn't be working with
- focuses on the past (what's worked and what hasn't), the present (the company's as well as the individual's current situation and goals), and the future (what the prospect's long-term plans are)
- focuses on the "how" and "why" of the three elements just listed (the past, present, and future)—how the prospect made the decision and why the current situation came about

Asking about the past, the present, and the future and focusing on the how and the why leads to extended conversations and a greater depth of sale. Asking the same tired boilerplate or "rapport-building" questions that everyone else is asking leads to briefer conversations, lost revenue opportunities, and reduced depth of sale.

Get into the habit of asking, "Why did you decide to go with XYZ Company?" or "How did you come to choose XYZ for your widget-cleaning service?"—and then listen carefully and take careful written notes of the answers you receive. These are essential strategies that support any attempt to develop a relationship based on interview-based selling techniques or to increase the value of an individual sale. And note that "Why did you decide to go with XYZ?" is a very different question from "Are you happy with XYZ?" or "What don't you like about XYZ?" Both of the latter questions leave you with nowhere to go and may tend to leave the prospect feeling uncomfortable.

The objective is to find out what the prospect is trying to get accomplished—not how he or she "feels" about the vendor in question! As you've no doubt already learned, even many prospects who tell reps that they hate a certain vendor do not take concrete action to change that vendor! So much for feelings!

Your subsequent questions should sound something like those that appear on the list below. Bear in mind that each prospect is different and that questions must be selected intelligently—not in a one-from-column-A, two-from-column-B fashion. Each question you ask should reflect your commitment to exploring new areas of mutual benefit.

- How many people work here?
- How many people in your department use widgets as a regular part of their job?
- Who do you think uses widgets the most in your department?
- What kind of work are you personally trying to get accomplished on the average day?

- What other companies does your firm own?
- What's on the horizon for your company/department/team?

Do you know who the company's primary customers are? What the main business goal of your contact is? What the company's expansion plans are? If you aren't getting this kind of information, then you're not getting the most out of the interview process!

Before the first meeting, jot down at least ten things you want to know about the prospect. Then examine each question and ask yourself how you could use this question to explore the ideas of the prospect's past, present, or future. How could you turn this into a question that begins with the word "how" or "why"?

BY THE WAY . . .

"By the way" may just be the three most important words in the world of sales. These words allow you to resume control of a conversation without overwhelming the prospect and to initiate a two-way dialogue about the prospect's current objectives. Here are some examples:

By the way, what other telecommunications services are you currently using?

By the way, how do your employees communicate with each other?

By the way, how does your president keep in touch with the central office when he travels?

As you use the ideas in this chapter to establish your own effective interviewing techniques, remember that a good interviewer

- is genuinely interested
- is curious
- really cares
- doesn't presume that the prospect "needs" anything, including the products or services that the interviewer represents

The four steps that allow you to lead or take charge of a sale are (1) ask, (2) listen, (3) learn, and then (and only then) (4) offer to help. (This offer marks the shift into the presentation phase. It may take you several meetings to reach this point.)

Before you walk out the door at the conclusion of your first meeting, you should determine whether or not the prospect is still playing ball with you. We'll look at exactly how to do that in the next chapter.

30

SECOND MEETINGS,
SECOND CONTACTS

One of the most important things you can do is make sure that you're talking with the right person. There are a number of ways to do this. One of the most effective (and indispensable) is to make a specific request for a second appointment before you walk out the door from your first meeting. Your request might sound like this:

Mr. Smith, I've learned a lot from our conversation, and I think we ought to keep looking at this. I'd like to take some time to review the notes I've taken here today, jot down some ideas on how we might work together, and review those with you. Could we do that next Thursday at two?

In other words, you want to "ratchet up" the relationship. You want to make an overt, specific attempt to schedule a second meeting—this time, perhaps, with an expert in tow. That "expert" could be your company's software designer, or it could be a consultant you've worked with, or it could be your brother-in-law. Your objective now is to determine whether or not this prospect is willing to invest more time and energy in discussing possible solutions with you, preferably with another person in attendance. In a great many cases, your prospect will start hedging and will give you important information you need to take into account.

The conversation might go something like this: "Actually, any decision on new widget-maintenance purchases would have to go by Harry in Operations," which leaves you perfectly positioned to say, "That's great—it sounds like you and I should meet with Harry. Let's go talk to Harry and see if we can set up a time."

Don't put off this step! Ratchet up the relationship *before* you head out the door. Ask to schedule that critical second appointment *before* you leave the first one. Make your request specific; make it focused; make it direct. Don't leave things up in the air.

What better time is there to gauge the actual level of commitment of your contact? And what have you got to lose by asking? If you can't win a formal appointment at the close of the first meeting, try to follow up by phone to find out when you can next get together with your contact(s) or, at the very least, to find out what has to happen *before* you can schedule that second meeting. But by all means *try* to establish that next meeting. A prospect who still fails to make any commitment to spend more time with you—despite your efforts after the fact—is, in all likelihood, a poor time investment for you, no matter how well the first meeting went!

Let me make that point as clear as possible: A first meeting that goes magnificently but does not result at some point in a firm commitment for a second meeting is unlikely to turn into a sale for you! Don't fall into the trap of rating your prospects by how pleasant they are to you during the initial meeting. If your prospect is serious about doing business with you in the near future, he or she will agree, either at the end of the first meeting or shortly thereafter, to a second session.

A prospect who will not commit to *any* "next step" with you

is not someone you should be spending time, energy, attention, or your organization's money pursuing. That prospect
is now a low-percentage candidate for future business, a fallback. After you've tried two or perhaps three times to set up
the next appointment by phone, give yourself a break and the
other person a rest. Wait a month or two; then call back to
see what's up. But *don't* waste your time blizzarding this person with faxes, messages, or correspondence. Make your final
appeal; then move on to someone new.

Suppose the person agrees to meet with you again, without
any hesitation? You're still going to want to ascertain that
you're talking to the right person. One of the biggest mistakes
you can make is to assume that the person who meets with
you initially is the only person involved in the decision to
work with you. In some cases, you're going to want to ask
your prospect a question like, "How did you decide to go with
XYZ Company?" The answer you get to that question is likely
to give you some meaningful information about who's involved in the decision-making process. If your contact has no
clue who's in charge of these decisions, that's a sign that you
need to ask him or her to help you set up a meeting with
someone else in the organization. Don't make the mistake of
asking, "Are you involved in making this decision?" because
the person will almost invariably say, "Yes, it's me. I'm in
charge."

From the facts-of-life department: Especially early on in
the relationship, you're going to encounter people who say
that they're in charge of things that they're not really in
charge of. That's not because they're out to mislead you or
because the prospect is fundamentally dishonest. It's because
the relationship with your prospect is still young.

The less experience you have with someone, the less likely
you are to pass along accurate information to that person. If
you think about it, that's the way you probably treat tele-
marketers who ask you, "Have you ever subscribed to such-
and-such a magazine?" There's no real impetus for you to
give them a detailed chronology of your entire magazine-

subscription-buying history. But if your brother-in-law asked you that question, you would probably provide better data.

So there's a reliable rule for you: The older the relationship, the better the information. The younger the relationship, the worse the information. The more time you spend with someone, the more likely you are to get accurate facts about what he or she does and what the organization's goals are. In fact, that's one of the main reasons you want to get more people involved, to say, "You know, I'd like to have my technical person meet with your technical person next week," even if that second meeting may not result in more specific technical data for you to work with. Such a meeting does, however, give you the chance to move the relationship forward to the next level, to deepen and improve the quality of the information that you'll be getting in the long run. And it is, as I say, a great opportunity to meet new decision makers within the target company, gauge the interest level in what you have to offer, and confirm (or revise) key assumptions from your first meeting.

The second appointment is by far the most difficult one to get. Just about anybody can get a first appointment, but once you get a commitment from your prospect to, for instance, let you bring your technical person in to speak with the other side's technical person, or perhaps to bring someone else in your organization in to talk with a senior executive at the target company, you know for sure that the other side is still playing ball.

Notes are even more important in meetings with two or more people than they are in your initial meeting, and I can't overemphasize the importance of taking carefully detailed notes throughout the sales process. During the second meeting, you might restate all the main assumptions you developed from the first meeting about objectives, obstacles, and past history. Make sure you jot down everything people have to say about these assumptions! You want to be sure, as the second meeting moves forward, that you're getting everything down about who said what, who appears to be in formal charge of what, and who appears to be in *actual* charge of what.

As the sales process moves forward, you're going to use all of your information—which is, you must remember, steadily increasing in quality—to develop a preliminary presentation. This is not *the* presentation. It's an insurance policy, and it may be the single most important element of your entire customized marketing effort.

We'll talk about this precursor to your formal proposal in the next chapter.

31

THE PRELIMINARY PROPOSAL

The assumption I'll make from this point on is that you've developed a fairly good relationship with your prospect and you've moved on to your second or third meeting with this person. You've listened. You've taken careful notes. You've met with all the key people in the organization who have input with regard to decisions about what you have to offer. There's no doubt about it—this prospect is playing ball with you—working with you to move the sales cycle forward.

At this point, you may be tempted to move forward to the formal presentation portion of the cycle. That is, you may want to sit down with the prospect, pass along your formal written proposal, and start talking in detail about all the wonderful things you can do for that person or that organization. But I'm going to ask you to do yourself and your prospect a favor by holding off. Before you start making formal recommendations, you will want to make sure that the prospect has had sufficient input into the process and that he or she is in agreement with each and every assumption you've made and each and every suggestion you're about to make.

Rather than make a single all-or-nothing appeal to your prospect, you're going to ask for a meeting at which he or she will review your *preliminary* proposal. In essence, this is a document designed to be corrected, a condensed summary of all the key facts and recommendations you'll be expanding on in your formal proposal. The idea here is not simply to get the prospect to look at your document, nod once or twice vigorously, and say, "Looks fine to me," but to encourage him or her to write down questions, comments, and concerns on the draft you've brought along.

You might precede your discussion about the preliminary proposal by saying something like the following to your prospect:

> Mr. Smith, here's what I was talking about on the phone; this is a rough outline of the material we're planning to use for our formal proposal. Before we go ahead and set up that final proposal, though, I wanted to give you the chance to review everything we'd assembled here, and I wanted to get some feedback from you on some aspects of the service we're discussing. Take a look and let me know what you think, particularly of Section III, which talks about core objectives.

No preliminary proposal can serve as a model for every business situation. Your preliminary proposal should reflect not what you have to say but what your prospective customer has to say. Remember all those notes you were taking during the interview phase? You're going to want to use as many verbatim quotes about the prospect's goals, philosophy, and requirements as you can in this document! Here are some general guidelines on what your preliminary proposal should look like:

It should be brief, but not too brief. Any longer than three or four pages is probably a mistake because relying on a long document will reduce the amount of meaningful feedback you receive. Any shorter than three or four pages is probably a mistake because the prospect will tend to "breeze through" the document and may not take it seriously.

It should be unique. Don't assume that the same material you used to win over one customer will do the trick when dealing with another customer. Customize the preliminary proposal to the needs of the organization; use words and phrases that you've noted during your interviews.

It should not go into too much detail. Don't overwhelm the prospect with technical material. Cover the key points the prospect has raised in the past—perhaps by organizing them under headings like "Assumptions," "Objective," "Methodology," "Overview," and "Benefits."

It should make brief reference to successful programs or products you've delivered for others. But beware—you must not allow your references to successful experiences with other companies to become an excuse for turning the preliminary proposal into a one-size-fits-all document. The name of the game is customization, so you should probably keep your references to previous happy customers or former work associates to a sentence or two.

It should offer some sense of the price and time lines involved. If budget or scheduling issues are a problem, you'll want to address that now—rather than during your formal presentation. Many entrepreneurs choose to accompany the written preliminary presentation with a verbal estimate of the general price ranges under discussion.

It should be attractive. Bind it neatly, and make sure there are no typographical errors or layout mistakes. Save the snazzy color graphics for the longer, formal document; including them here may discourage your prospect from writing on the document, which is what you want him or her to do.

It should verify all the key information you've developed in your interview. This is one of the most important aspects of your preliminary proposal; it represents your last chance to ferret out inaccurate or misunderstood data.

It should not *attempt to close out issues still under discus-*

sion. Your aim is to get the prospect to think, "Oh, wait, that's right—we still have to finalize so-and-so." Any attempt to railroad your way through important questions will probably backfire.

In the final analysis, the objective of the preliminary written proposal is to help you identify and address any objections that still remain *before* you move on to your final presentation. Ideally, of course, you would have discussed everything of consequence during your interview phase, but ours is not an ideal world. The preliminary proposal allows you, in a low-pressure environment, to examine any remaining obstacles to doing business together. If the preliminary proposal indicates that you've got more interviewing or research to do, you're not ready to move on to the presentation phase!

By the time you've finished with the review of your preliminary proposal, the following should be true:

- The prospect should have given you detailed written—or, at the very least, verbal—feedback about the material you've included in your preliminary presentation.
- The prospect should understand that you will be basing your formal presentation on the preliminary presentation he or she has just reviewed.
- The prospect should have given you some sign of assent. (This could be a statement like, "Looks good to me" or "I think you've got it all covered.")
- The prospect should understand that you intend to ask for a formal business commitment during your next meeting.
- The prospect should have agreed to a specific date and time for your next meeting, with all appropriate decision makers in attendance.

If each of the above conditions has been met—congratulations! You're ready to move on to the presentation phase. If even one of the above elements is missing—you are not as far ahead in the process as you thought you were. You're not ready to move to the presentation yet; you need to gather more information.

A final word of caution about the preliminary proposal: Don't let the length of the document fool you! This is one of the most important elements of your entire person-to-person marketing campaign. Although it will only be three to four pages in length, this is definitely one of those projects that it is worth your while to peruse carefully. Develop several drafts; make sure your preliminary proposal addresses all the key issues, clearly outlines the main elements of what you can do, and "speaks the prospect's language."

32

WINNING COMMITMENT

The formal presentation you deliver should prominently feature key information derived from the prospect during the interview phase and verified by the conclusion of that phase. To the degree that the presentation incorporates words and phrases from the prospect's work environment, it's likely to succeed. To the degree that it sounds "uncustomized," it's likely to fail!

With accurate, verified information, the presentation phase is likely to look very familiar to the prospect. All the key points and concerns from the interview phase should be addressed as the prospect directed and, preferably, in the prospect's own language.

If the prospect sees something new during the presentation that he or she doesn't like, there's a problem. Remember, the prospect should know that you're planning to ask for a formal business commitment before you begin your presentation.

Your formal presentation should be practiced ahead of time.

It should cover familiar ground. Don't introduce elements that were not covered at all in your preliminary proposal. Expand on what appeared there.

It should be delivered both verbally and on paper. As a practical matter, your audience will be listening to you and referring, from time to time, to the written document you have supplied.

It should use visual aids to win interest and attention. The written element of your presentation should probably include some form of color illustration, at least on the first page.

It should go into considerably greater detail than the preliminary written proposal you developed. The actual length of your proposal will depend on the complexity of the project you're working on. Some prospects will require very long proposals indeed, which will be the basis of more concise verbal summaries.

It should have a spontaneous feel. You should incorporate as much eye contact as possible. The points you raise should not sound "canned" or prerehearsed.

It should outline pricing and scheduling options that you know or strongly suspect the prospect can live with. Once again: No surprises! Your earlier work should determine what you will outline during the proposal.

It should be geared to your audience's attention span. Don't bore people to tears! Keep the material upbeat and interesting, and don't drone on if you sense you're losing your audience. If you have doubts about the material's accessibility or the length of your presentation, consider practicing it in front of a friend or trusted colleague before you deliver it to your target audience. To talk longer than twenty minutes is usually dangerous.

It should offer proof. This might be a short demonstration of a piece of equipment, or a visual that features brief, enthusiastic quotes about your work.

It should offer a discussion of particular benefits. This might be a review of a key competitive advantage that what you have to offer will provide—improved sales totals, for instance.

It should offer a discussion of particular features. This might be a discussion of something special that you offer that someone else doesn't—for instance, a commitment to face-to-face service.

It should conclude with an unapologetic formal recommendation. It could sound like this: "Under the outline we're proposing, work would start very soon. We would begin on July sixteenth and complete the job no later than September first."

The conclusion of the presentation should move directly into the close: "Well, Mr. Smith, that's our proposal. I have to tell you—it makes sense to me. Does it make sense to you?" (That's the best closing technique I've ever heard of, by the way, and the only one I recommend for beginning entrepreneurs.) If you've done your work up to this point, the answer will, more often than not, be *yes*. Remember, you deliver your presentation *only* when you've received a "That sounds good to me" assent at the conclusion of the interview stage. This means that the transition to the request for business should not come as a surprise to your prospect!

If the answer you receive is *no*, guess what? There was an objection lurking somewhere, one that should have been evaluated and addressed during the interview stage! One of the best ways to get out of this dilemma (or for that matter, to address similar situations in the interview phase) is simply to take full responsibility for the problem. Instead of making excuses—or, even worse, complaining that the prospect has "misled" you—say something along the following lines:

> Ms. Jones, I have to apologize here. Obviously, I've done something wrong. We've looked at all the options, done all the research, and tried to come up with the very best approach for you—and I know for a fact that the widgets we're discussing are the very best on the market. So if what we're proposing

now doesn't make sense, the only explanation I can come up with is that I must have made a serious mistake at some point. I'd like to ask you a favor—can you tell me where I went wrong, what I did that took this off course for you?

By assuming "blame" in this way, you encourage the prospect to show you exactly where the problem was. In all likelihood, Ms. Jones will say,

No, no, Jerry, it's not you—it's our accounting people. We've just learned that we have to go through some much more stringent purchasing procedures than we've ever had to deal with before. If I'd known about the new guidelines when we met last week, I would have brought them up then. But rest assured that the problem is not on your end.

If the prospect says this—or any of the possible variations of the New Objection You Wish You'd Uncovered Earlier— you'll at least have a better idea of where you stand with this target company. You may have more work to do, but you won't be doing it in the dark. So, be ready to assume personal responsibility for the sale, and never be afraid to be "corrected" if doing so will give you a realistic chance of developing more information.

In most cases, however, if you follow the advice I've laid out here and in previous chapters, you won't run into too many situations where you encounter brand-new objections during the presentation phase. If you use the system we've been discussing, the presentation should lead naturally to a formalization of your business relationship with the prospect. Be honest, be direct, be straightforward, help the prospect visualize what you're saying, and be conversational. You'll then be in a great position to move forward in the relationship.

You may have noticed that this book features no separate chapter on closing techniques. That's because I strongly believe the vast majority of these techniques to be a complete waste of time! Only a determined effort to build a solid, mutually beneficial business relationship can result in a new business commitment. If you skip that part, it doesn't much matter what you say at the end of the process. If you don't skip that part, a simple confirmation—"This really makes sense to me—what do you think?"—is more than sufficient.

For a full review of some alternate ways to approach the "It makes sense to me" close, you may want to take a look at my book *High-Efficiency Selling*. In the vast majority of cases, however, the strategy I've provided here will see you through just fine.

33

MONITORING THE SOLUTIONS YOU DELIVER

It's important to keep in mind that once you sell your product or service to someone, you want to follow up and meet personally with your contact and find out what worked and what didn't. The simple act of posing the question "How are things working out?" will go a long way toward ensuring harmonious relations with your customers.

There's a tendency to think of customer-service matters as low-level work. Actually, for businesses that plan to survive—and that definitely includes a small business you're launching yourself—customer-service work is the most important work you can do. After all, for many entrepreneurs the question of how to secure repeat business is one of the most important issues of the day. What has more effect on that issue than customer service?

Just as there is no replacement for the "head honcho" serving as salesperson during the early years of the business, I would argue that there's no better customer-service person during this period than someone who knows all aspects of the business intimately. You simply can't afford slipups in customer service during the first year or two of operation.

There will, of course, be slipups and misunderstandings; the question is, How will you respond to them? Your attitude and your willingness to accept responsibility will usually make all the difference. Just as people respond in kind during the sales cycle, they will respond in kind during their relationship with you as your customer. That means that a bored, uninformed, or unmotivated employee can wreak havoc on your relationship with a given customer and, by extension, on your entire operation. A major customer problem that's addressed forthrightly, honestly, and with the same attentive, open, nonjudgmental attitude with which you opened the sales relationship can lay the foundation for a great deal of repeat business in the future. A minor problem that's addressed rudely, insensitively, or with no concern for the business interests of the other side can do irreparable harm to a relationship.

The best strategy for effective one-on-one customer-service improvement is to focus on building the relationship first— and to realize that the majority of problems people face in their dealings with companies are never acknowledged by the companies, much less resolved to the customer's satisfaction. So if there was a screwup, be willing to admit there was a screwup. That doesn't necessarily mean you'll do anything and everything to retain even a customer who represents only a small amount of revenue to your firm, but it does mean you should be willing, when circumstances warrant it, to say those magic words: "I'm sorry. We made a mistake." That's taking the personal-responsibility approach discussed in the previous chapters to its logical conclusion.

Customers love it when someone is willing to step forward and acknowledge that a problem exists, apologize for it, and set up a clear plan of action to help resolve it and make sure that it doesn't come up in the future. You have to be willing to tell a customer, "You're right—we did misship your order,

and I want to apologize personally to you. I'll set up a dupli-
cate order today." When you can make that commitment—
either during the customer's call to you or during a promptly
placed follow-up call—you're focusing in on relationship-
building.

The more distinctive the personal touch you can offer during your contacts with customers, the happier both of you
will be. I know of a great many small firms that build up intense loyalty in their customer base by making a point of talking about everyday triumphs and obstacles. When a customer
calls up to ask about an order, the entrepreneur might ask
who the gift purchase is for. If it's for a daughter, the entrepreneur might mention the fact that she has a daughter ap-
proximately the same age. When was the last time a
customer-service representative at HugeCorp took the time
to draw a personal parallel like that with someone who called
in on the 800 line?

When you handle problems yourself, particularly on key
accounts, you're taking the opportunity to let the person
know that in marked contrast to what might happen with a
much larger business, where a customer-service problem
might sit in a file system for months or even years, you're
willing to take strong action quickly, to develop a plan that
will help ensure that the problem won't arise again, and to
make a personal guarantee to that effect if you can and if it's
appropriate to do so. That's the kind of behavior that many
large businesses can't match—and that wins repeat business
for small businesses like yours!

And while we're on the subject of problem resolution—why
wait for the problem to develop in the first place? I strongly
suggest that you develop the habit of calling or meeting with
your customers—or at the very least, your key customers—on
a regular basis. The idea here is not to try to sell them on
products or services you offer, but simply to keep in touch, to
see how things are going, and to offer your personal thanks
for doing business with your firm.

At DEI we make a habit of phoning current customers on

a regular basis—once every six months or so. This is in addition to whatever prospecting or follow-up work we're doing with the customer. We make a point of calling up at least twice a year and saying, "Hey, we just want to thank you for doing business with us, and we hope that all is going well, and we want to find out how things are going with you and how the program is working out." We're able to identify little problems before they become big problems and enhance our relationships with our customer base. That's a tradition I started many years ago, and it has paid handsome dividends over the years.

You get some great feedback with this method; and even though these calls aren't marketing calls per se, they have the strange effect of leading to quite a lot of add-on business for our firm—sometimes from people who haven't done business with us for months and weren't planning to until we called! The attentive follow-up call reminded them how seriously we took our commitment to deliver positive results. That's an advantage you should be putting to work for your business, too.

Crisis!

How do you handle a customer crisis? If you are dealing with a key account who's got a real difficulty with the product or service you've provided, then it's definitely in everyone's best interest, and certainly yours, to schedule a face-to-face meeting with this person. If necessary, go through all the phases that you went through in the selling cycle: Take all the notes, figure out what's working and what's not, and develop a preliminary or final proposal that will resolve the problem to the customer's satisfaction—at no charge. That's a great way to build relationships. When you show that you put the same amount of attentiveness and care and interest and insight into resolving a problem with the current customer that you did during the "courtship" period, you make a very strong positive statement about your business as a whole.

It's important not to take these steps thoughtlessly, however. As I've alluded to earlier in this book, some people are net drains on your time, energy, and attention, and always will be. You have to bear in mind that not all customers are equal—some have a potential value that's significantly greater than that of others. Which customer will you spend your time with?

Your time is one of your most critical assets while starting your own business, and you have to be careful not to spend three or four days' worth of your own time resolving a problem for a customer who represents $50 to your firm and, in the process, neglecting a customer who represents $1,500 to your firm, or $2,000 or $10,000 or $100,000! There are certain steps you're going to take with key customers that you might not take with customers who do not fall into that category. And it's important to remember, too, that of the people who reach you and who ask to do business with you, there is going to be a small percentage who make life very difficult, who are never going to be satisfied with anything you do, and who represent a very small dollar value to you.

These days, it's popular to talk about the importance of superior customer service for each and every customer of a company, and it is certainly a very laudable goal to deliver the highest quality of customer service possible to everyone you come in contact with. But it is also important to recognize that you can't be everything to everyone.

So you have to approach these customer-service issues with a sense of balance and restraint and understanding. There are some people for whom complaining is a way of life and who will see their decision to purchase a $10 gift from you as an invitation to regale you with hour upon hour upon hour of complaints. There's going to come a point at which it's just not worth it to try to resolve every problem that a particular customer brings to your attention. It's better to determine what that point is early on in the exchange, rather than later, so you can disengage tactfully and then talk to other people who really can benefit from what you have to offer.

PART

IV

GROWING UP

I remember years ago a major account of mine, a retailer with twenty-four stores, asked me how my business was. I said, "I think it's going fairly well." He said, "Well, how did you do last month compared to this month?" And I said, "Gee, I don't know. I actually hadn't thought about it."

He took out an index card from his wallet, and there he had the actual income he had made from last year to this year. And he tracked that; he knew exactly how much money he did each month for each one of the stores. He carried that with him so he could analyze it and think about it and ponder what he needed to do to improve.

From that point on, I started carrying a similar index card. And, to this day, each month I go through an elaborate exercise of analyzing my sales and analyzing exactly what I have booked to date, what I have booked that needs to be completed, and how much money needs to be collected. I'm also religious about tracking my cash flow and my pending receivables. You should be, too!

There comes a point in your growth when you realize you have to change your way of looking at things. Perhaps you need to monitor financial issues more closely or you have to expand or you have to set up new personnel systems or you have to develop new relationships with key customers. That discussion with my retail customer was one of those transition moments for me. In this part of the book, we'll look at some other signs of change in your business and suggest how you should respond to them.

34

MANAGERS:
BEING ONE, HIRING ONE

Things are looking up. Your personal marketing campaign has been paying off. A year or two has passed; it's finally time to start looking at expanding your sales department from one person (you) to several people. What does it take to be a sales manager? And what do you need in the person you hire to manage your sales force, if you decide to hand that job over to someone else?

Many entrepreneurs, myself included, tend to keep active in some form of sales supervisory activity, even when new sales personnel come on board. Perhaps they let their presence at selected appointments "up the ante." Not long ago, our company secured an account with a major investment firm, in large measure because I showed up for the meeting! The CEO asked me, "Why on earth are you here?" I answered, "Because I care about this project a great deal, and I want everything to work out well for you." He was impressed.

By the way, that's an important function of the sales man-

ager, whether it's you or someone else, to occasionally accompany a sales rep on an appointment to signal interest and
investment to the prospective buyer. Beyond that, the real
work you have to do as a manager, and the responsibility of
any manager that you hire, is to develop your people. You
need to help them to grow, to improve their selling skills (the
ones in Part III that you yourself developed) and to develop
professionally. For their part, they need to take ownership of
their sales objectives and to feel a personal and professional
commitment to taking whatever actions are necessary in a
given situation. Whoever acts as your sales manager, this is
the work that will have the greatest effect on the productivity
of your team.

I don't believe that sales managers can really motivate
salespeople. Salespeople have to motivate themselves. Your
job and the job of any sales manager that you hire is to find
or create situations in which they can develop the potential
that's already within them. You can and should provide a cli-
mate of growth for your people. This involves not just money
and job security, but a lot of little things—for instance, helping your people through your company's red tape when a sale
is hanging in the balance and discussing and reaching realistic sales objectives by mutual agreement, not simply by assigning arbitrary goals. Attention, individual recognition,
credit for a job well done, personal interest in their families,
these are the things that make salespeople feel like part of the
team and make them likely to motivate themselves.

With your new people, you use coaching sessions to gain
their trust and help them to reach beyond their limits. With
your experienced people, a coaching session can be used to
further sharpen skills and to develop new management-
related strengths for the future. Coaching is a powerful way
of communicating with your people and supplying the necessary feedback (positive and negative) to help your salespeople
grow and reach their full potential. Coaching is also part of
the problem-solving process. If something is happening that
shouldn't be, or something isn't happening that should be,

the sales manager needs to go through the basic steps of problem solving—that is, define the problem, decide what to do, and take action. Coaching ensures that your people know that management is on their side, that their needs are understood, and that you want to help them grow. This builds the atmosphere of trust necessary for high productivity.

Coaching often takes the form of role-playing, with you or your salespeople as your "customers." In other situations, you'll be trying to "sell" a technique, a skill, a goal, or a concept. A good sales manager will focus his or her coaching on two areas: (1) sales skills—improving sales performance by explaining, demonstrating, and providing practice in various skills of the selling process, such as communication, precall planning, strategy development, team planning, follow-up, and so on; (2) work habits—improving performance by correcting poor work habits, such as lateness or incompleteness of sales reports. Sometimes poor work habits are the result of an inability to apply skills correctly; sometimes they reflect a larger problem. In practice, making a distinction between these two areas of coaching shouldn't matter as much as simply doing whatever is within the sales manager's power to improve the salesperson's situation through a coaching session.

A good sales manager must also be adept at recognizing those situations in which a coaching session will not be appropriate or effective—for example, the case of a salesperson who is unwilling or unable to recognize or "own" the particular problem, or has a personal problem beyond the control of a nonprofessional (for example, substance abuse). The sales manager cannot play psychiatrist and is expected to recognize when he or she lacks expertise to handle a problem.

Any sales manager has the overall responsibility of seeing to it that the sales force achieves the company's goals. But a sales manager can't be concerned only with the numbers. There also has to be concern for the ongoing development of the people who work for the company. Developing people is largely a communication process, just like the art of selling itself. You have to use the same basic communication skills when interacting with your people that they use in working with customers. You must commit to building relationships, just as you would with an important customer. And as you communicate over time, you have to develop a shared terminology with your salespeople—and with your sales manager—that will enable you to work together with a minimum of misunderstanding.

Therefore, in addition to a record of demonstrated achievement, communication skills will be a major requirement for a candidate when it comes time to hire a sales manager to oversee or recruit your sales staff. And that time will surely come as your company grows beyond your ability to wear a number of different hats. As your company's owner and CEO, you will eventually have to learn how to delegate—how to outline the essentials of a task to a qualified person, step back, and get out of the way.

Often, that means hiring a sales manager, somebody who will run things as you wish to see them run and who clearly demonstrates the ability to develop people and help them grow according to the motivational forces inside of them. Knowing how well your potential sales manager can interact with others—clearly communicate his or her thoughts, use the strategies you've learned in this book, and help a sales rep to achieve his or her full potential—is crucial to the success of your company. If your sales manager cannot create an environment in which his or her people are encouraged to be good communicators themselves, then it's time to look for another manager!

Of course, since salespeople are trained to be communicators, how do you determine that the person you are hiring to be your sales manager is able to sell not only a product or service, but the techniques and goals of productive salesmanship to his or her staff? Well, like any other hiring process, it's a crapshoot to some extent. Some people are very good at selling themselves, but very poor at doing the job. Sometimes you won't really know what you've got until the person is on the premises and demonstrating his or her capabilities. So sometimes it's a matter of judging the situation after the hiring, and determining then whether you have struck gold—or lead. This is one reason why many companies insist on a probationary period of, say, ninety days, before extending a permanent offer of employment. This is a strategy you may want to consider employing in any hiring situation—not just situations that are sales related. (Appendix B features a list of interview questions you will probably want to review before making any full-time hire.)

One way to discover whether you have hired the right person for the sales manager's job is by sitting in on a coaching session and making a checklist of what your manager is or is not able to do. Some questions you might want to ask yourself include:

- Was the purpose of the session clearly stated at the outset?
- Did your manager focus on "what works" by starting and ending with positive reinforcement?
- Was the salesperson asked to describe the situation?
- Did your manager listen, ask questions, and observe with an open mind?
- Was the manager able to develop the salesperson's sense of his or her part in the evaluation of the situation?
- Were problems examined as opportunities for future growth?
- When an agreement on action to be taken was reached, was it mutual and was it verified to ensure that both parties understood and accepted it?
- Were explanations brief and to the point?
- Were recommendations tailored to the salesperson's sales objectives?
- Did the manager know—and clearly explain—his or her expectations?
- Did the salesperson make a clear commitment to the plan of action?

- Was a mutually agreeable follow-up date set to ensure commitment and compliance with the plan?

You may also be able to determine your candidates' ability to satisfy these questions by talking to others with whom the candidate has worked. Nose around. Ask questions. It isn't enough to have somebody who knows how to sell. You also have to have somebody who knows how to lead.

For that matter, you may have the sales manager you need right in front of you. Don't be afraid to mine your own sales force for those who may be ready to move up to management. Remember, you want a good communicator, and if that means taking somebody with less actual managerial experience—well, you might be better off! In this regard, I would caution you not to focus solely on the high achievers who emerge in your sales force. The superstars of selling may not necessarily be the superstars of managing. Often the people who can show steady, trustworthy performances, somewhere in the middle of overall sales achievements, are those who are the best equipped in many ways to take over the management of a sales team. So don't overlook your middle achievers—they may be your best asset!

Just as your salespeople need coaching, so do your sales managers. They should be fully versed in what you expect of them, what they need to achieve, and how they can use their skills to achieve the goals you set for them. You, for your part, must always be providing the feedback they need to reach this understanding and to review their progress and achievement of goals. Remember, even when you are no longer the sales manager yourself, you are still a manager. You must always be doing what you can to cultivate an atmosphere of growth and to develop your people's full potential—as well as meet sales goals, of course!

35

WHY GROWTH IS EXPENSIVE

What is the most desirable cause of a big increase in your business expenses? In a word—success!

The more successful you are, the more likely you are to need to spend additional money in order to keep up with the growth of your business. Changes in technology and changes in the marketplace may also impact your every move: In time you may need to buy new software, new equipment, new systems. You will need to hire more employees to handle increased business. You will need to provide training to your sales staff, perhaps bring in consultants to evaluate your business and suggest improvements. More legal paperwork will need to be processed, meaning more billable hours of your attorney's time. Accounting procedures will have to be adjusted, upgrades to current systems implemented to keep up with the latest developments. The more successful you are, the more you will need to spend—it's as simple as that.

But success can be deceptive. It can trick you into thinking the money to make improvements is there in bucketfuls when, in fact, you have to be just as attentive to costs as you were when you started the business—perhaps even more so. Care has to be taken that you don't spread yourself—and your available capital—too thin. With each improvement that you make, with each new person that you hire, you have to ensure that you are properly prepared and that your company's finances can absorb the impact of increased expenses. Every dollar that you spend must be justifiable.

Too often, small-business owners get heady with their success. As the profit margin widens, so does the tendency to indulge oneself. You might think to yourself, "I'm doing so well, I can afford to buy that wonderful widgetmaster I've heard so much about." But how necessary is that widgetmaster to your business? What will it do to help increase your profits? Is it a justifiable expense or merely an indulgence?

When you started up your business, you were probably careful to manage every penny, to determine exactly how much you needed to spend, how many people you could afford to hire, whether buying or leasing equipment would work best for you, and so forth. This vigilance and attention to detail cannot let up for a moment! By the same token, without the people to handle the increased workload, you and your current staff will become burned out and won't function efficiently or effectively. Without the right hardware and software, you won't be able to keep up with the competition. Without the necessary adjustments to changes in the industry, your business will never be able to survive past the first stage of success.

So what do you do? How do you achieve this fine balance between increasing spending and keeping expenses under control? For starters, you need to have the right financial manager for your business. Seeing that your company's finances are managed effectively as you grow should clearly be one of your highest priorities as a small-business owner. If you haven't secured the advice of a qualified financial professional up to this point, you will certainly want to strongly consider doing so before you start a major expansion plan.

Sometimes companies can grow so fast that their owners fail to build in the necessary safeguards that keep the finances under control. A business that starts out with one or two people, who have only basic skills, handling the financial end of things cannot be expected to continue functioning with this arrangement after the company has grown dramatically. What works for a start-up does not necessarily work for the same company three or four years down the line. If the financial controls aren't there, then the company may develop cash-flow problems that can turn your burgeoning business into a nightmare.

Thus, you need to ensure that the financial responsibility for the company is assumed by an experienced and skilled employee who will report on a regular basis to you, the owner, and keep your company's management fully informed about and involved in the monitoring of the finances. Whether this person is a bookkeeper, an accountant, or a chief financial officer, you must have enough confidence in his or her skills and competency to know that your company will be overseen with the same care you yourself took when you first started.

Any growth has to be handled with care. If your revenues balloon, so will the temptation to spend. Even if your growth isn't explosive, if you decide to expand, you should go at it slowly. Know what the market demand is: Will it accommodate your decision to produce twice the number of widgets you currently make, or will you end up with surplus inventory that you will have to write off as a loss? Thorough market research is crucial to planning any expansion. So is knowing what your staff can or cannot handle.

Say, for example, that you're doing so well in your novelty-toy business that you decide to double your product line. Your salespeople now have more to offer your customers, and the response is strongly favorable. Orders double practically overnight. But production costs are such that you can't afford to hire any more employees for your customer-service department.

The existing staff suddenly has double the workload they had before, and no systems are in place to accommodate the increase in business. Because they have more work than they can handle, your employees begin to fall behind on orders—and on responding to increasingly numerous customer complaints. They have no incentive to work harder, because you can't afford salary increases. Thus, morale falls, and turnover increases as burned-out workers leave for less pressured work environments.

It takes time to train new staff. This affects productivity and sales as customers become disgruntled due to your staff's inattentiveness and lack of response. In time your customers start taking their business elsewhere because they're not getting the satisfaction they want or need from your company. Sales fall—and you're back where you started.

Every step that you take in expanding your business can have that kind of domino effect. Each division interacts with others, so any change in one division is likely to have some impact on another division. All of this must be taken into account when you expand. You also have to consider the impact on you that expansion will have. You put in many long hours at the beginning to set up your company and get it off the ground. If you're working twice as hard now just to keep it in the air, then maybe you've gone about it the wrong way.

You can't continually inflict stress on yourself, your staff, and your company's finances. Profitability should be a result, not of superhuman sacrifice, but of careful planning—anticipating what you will need, knowing what you can afford to spend and what your employees can handle, having proper financial management—in other words, attention to the details and a mania for watching expenses.

Where are your biggest expenses likely to be found? According to a recent Dun and Bradstreet survey, a whopping twenty-eight percent of your total income from sales is likely to go to compensating your employees, with an additional four percent going toward employee benefits. Fifteen percent pays your taxes. Expenses associated with sales and marketing consume nine percent. Surprisingly, you should generally expect only about three percent of your revenues to be lost to bad debt.

This means you can reasonably expect that the more employees you have, the more you are going to be spending on compensation and benefits. This can eat into revenues so much, in fact, that many small-business owners who are trying to save their flagging business find it necessary to lay off full-time employees. One way to hold on to your employees while keeping compensation costs under control is to provide monetary incentives that enable you to keep salaries relatively low. For example, any employee who comes up with a cost-cutting idea that works could be paid a bonus out of the resulting savings (say, five to twenty percent of his or her base pay). Other incentives might include employee recognition days, plenty of praise, and providing opportunities for advancement.

Many small-business owners choose not to provide health insurance to employees as a way of keeping costs down. If you choose to go this route, keep in mind that you will be much less likely to attract good employees, as the best talent will undoubtedly opt to go to a company where benefits are offered. This could potentially leave you with the problem of having an even greater workload in the long run because of turnover and inept help, which may in itself be expensive. This is not to say that you should be matching the benefits packages offered by larger firms; but you should at least try to stay in line with what other small businesses are offering. (Similarly, you can minimize costs by limiting the amount of insurance you buy, but this too has risks.)

Another possibility for keeping down employee-related costs, to which I've already alluded in an earlier chapter, is to hire temporary workers. You would not be paying them benefits, and they could be brought in to handle any extra workload resulting from explosive growth and dismissed when they are no longer needed or you're finally in a position to hire permanent employees. You can also outsource professional services, such as legal and accounting work, or hire freelancers or subcontractors to do certain jobs. These options can be especially helpful in the early years of your company's operation.

Aside from employee-related costs, another major expense may occur when you upgrade technology that you use, especially if what you were using to "make do" becomes so obsolete that your business suffers. In the case of some small businesses, the necessary technology takes a huge bite out of revenues, and often this can be the largest contributor to any losses the company suffers in the early years.

As for taxes, although fifteen percent may seem high to you, the fact is that this is what many of the larger businesses also pay. You can't avoid the taxes, so you have no choice but to budget for them and look for other areas in which you can try to cut costs. For instance, you might put tighter controls on your inventory, leasing only as much space as you need to warehouse only as much inventory as you'll need to get you through a certain time frame (rather than overstocking). This requires careful planning and judgment but could save a great deal of money overall if done right.

The nine percent of revenues taken up by sales and marketing costs may prove to be a case of underspending, and certainly is not an area in which cost-cutting measures should be taken with any great vigor. Sales are the backbone of your company; your product or service does not, after all, sell itself. Yet many small businesses do not invest enough in their sales and marketing efforts. In particular, many experts point out, small businesses frequently underadvertise, when they should be advertising and promoting their products more vigorously.

When it comes to growth, you may find yourself caught between a rock and a hard place. On the one hand, without the proper financial controls, which may include cost-cutting measures, your company can grow too fast too soon, to the point where it's out of control. On the other hand, too much cost control can stifle your growth and be detrimental to future profitability. To truly handle the expense of expansion, it's important for you to keep your business on a slow but steady track, with able, talented people managing the finances and controls that save money but don't strangle the business in the process. Think of yourself as a jockey, with your business as your horse. You have to have the finest touch on the reins in order to give your mount its lead—and keep it on the track to success.

36

HOW TO HANDLE
A MARKET CRISIS

I remember one time, early on in my company's history, when I lost a major account. In fact, this account was about fifty percent of my business then. And so when the call came in that told me that this company was going to terminate its relationship with my firm, I was devasated! Half the business—vanished!

It can't be true, I thought to myself. I can't *let* it be true. So I went to see my contact in person. We took a walk together, and I almost came to the point of begging him to keep the account on. If I'd thought it would have helped I would probably have tried that. But the business was gone. There was no two ways about it. We shook hands as friends at the end of the meeting; he said, "Well, things may change and we'll call you back." I walked to the phone booth and called my accountant. My accountant, when I told him that I'd lost fifty percent of our year's business, said, "Well, Steve, if you had more accounts, you wouldn't be upset." After I fantasized ripping out his lungs, I realized how true that was. You need to always maintain an active base of prospects, which means you need to go out every day and sell.

I'd gotten complacent. I'd taken my eye off the ball. And now my "mother account" was gone.

What do you do when you find yourself in a situation like that? Well, here's what I did. If following these seven steps will help you make it through the kind of crisis I faced, then maybe what I went through was worthwhile after all.

STEP 1: *Don't panic.* Don't hyperventilate. Don't start circling ads in the classified section. Figure out what the worst-case scenario is and consider tapping any emergency financing sources (friends, relatives, banks, credit cards, whatever) that will help you make it through this period. If you start putting your energy and attention into developing a job-search campaign, there will be that much *less* energy that you'll be putting into the challenge of saving your business. You can't do both—so pick one. (Obviously, I picked trying to save my business.)

STEP 2: *Make up for lost time.* You've got some ground to make up, so get on the phone and start setting up appointments—fast. You may even want to consider hiring the best, most motivated, hungriest salesperson you can find who will work on a straight commission basis to help you develop new business. (I say "straight commission" because it's likely that you'll be in "survival mode" from a cash standpoint now. Even though you're less likely to wind up with a superior performer under this arrangement, if you select your candidate carefully, you will get something new on the prospect board—and that's the name of the game at this stage.)

STEP 3: *Apologize in advance to your family.* You're going to be putting in lots of nights and weekends for a while. They should understand this and be comfortable with it—or at least resigned to it.

STEP 4: *Consider new financing arrangements with new customers.* If you haven't been asking for a percentage of cash up front for the products or services you provide, this might be an excellent time to consider doing so.

STEP 5: *Slow down your payables.* Call key vendors and explain your situation; give them your best estimates of when you'll be able to resolve outstanding debts. Many of them are likely to be more understanding than you might at first expect.

When you've got your wits about you again, you can consider . . .

STEP 6: Remind yourself that *any business that relies* predominantly or exclusively *on a single account is inherently unstable,* and vow to continue to *expand your market base so that you'll never again be caught in this situation.*

STEP 7: *Take out a black felt-tip pen and a huge poster board and write the words "Prospecting Daily Equals Survival" on it in huge letters.* Leave the sign out where you can see it every time you sit down at your desk. You've survived the roller coaster once—you don't want to test the Fates to find out whether you can survive it a second time!

37

MANAGING YOUR BUSINESS
OVER THE LONG TERM

Are you in perpetual crisis mode?

When one fire after another needs putting out, day in and day out, you're in trouble. It's to be expected that some of the time something will go wrong; no business is without its downs as well as its ups. What you need to do is manage your company so that the ups outweigh the downs. This means knowing how to organize your business, knowing how to systemize your office, and knowing how to energize your staff.

If you've been following the advice and techniques offered in earlier sections of this book, then you should already have a good idea of what you need to know to organize your business. Above and beyond all else, you need a written strategy that will serve as your road map to meeting your goals (see Chapter 15, on developing your strategy map). Without a strong, effective plan, your company has no foundation on which to build to future success. A business plan stabilizes you, so that you know where you want to go, how you want to get there, and what progress you're making . You can't just get up each morning and decide, "For today I will run my business this way." That's just asking for trouble. You need structure; without it there can be no stability. Revise your written strategy once a year or at other intervals that seem appropriate to your business, but don't change it every day!

It's also important to be thoroughly knowledgeable about any changes in legal obligations and any other legal matters that may affect your business. As your business grows, it's entirely likely that you will need to seek out new professional allies for this area. What forms will you need to file, given recent changes in your business? What are your current tax issues? What do you now need in the way of insurance? What do you have to do now about copyrights, trademarks, and patents? These are just a few of the questions that often confront growing businesses. If your current legal or accounting help doesn't point you to the answers you need, you may want to consider augmenting the current team or changing it outright.

Managing your business means managing your staff. Without a competent work force, one that works together as a team, you are bound to be caught in a crisis-a-day syndrome that will drain both your own energies and those of the few good people you may have. An atmosphere of constant crises and pressure to get things done yesterday can also seriously affect employee morale. Your business must be managed in such a way as to have the lowest employee-turnover rate possible. You can't afford to be spending all of your time training new personnel because your old employees are always leaving you. This is neither cost-effective nor time-effective.

You also need to ensure that the necessary protection is in place to help you deal with unforeseen disasters. This includes being properly insured. Surprisingly, there is very little that is legally required for small-business owners to take out in the way of insurance, aside from workers' compensation and the possible insurance requirements when you rent office space. But you take enough risks as it is—you can't afford to have some calamity strike against which you are underinsured or, worse yet, not insured at all. This might have the effect of shutting your business down for good.

To avoid such a tragedy, make sure that you have what you need to truly protect your company and yourself. Eight insurance policies are available to small-business owners.

1. A *business owner's policy*, designed primarily for small service and manufacturing business, will provide wide coverage for a variety of needs, including property damage, injury liability, and interruption of your business. Policies are generally tailored to the particular business and usually do not cover professionals (that is, lawyers, accountants, consultants, and the like).

2. *Product liability insurance* provides protection if and when one of your products causes harm to its user. You should get this insurance if it's not covered in your business owner's policy and there's even the remotest risk of your product causing harm or damage in some way.

3. *Professional liability insurance* is not required by law, but it's a smart idea to get this coverage to protect yourself financially if somebody should bring suit against you for negligence or malpractice of any sort. This can be expensive insurance to buy and usually comes with limits on coverage and deductibles.

4. *Workers' compensation insurance* for all full-time and part-time employees is usually required. (Some states specify its necessity only for companies with three or more employees.) This covers your employees in the event of a work-related accident or illness. In some places, you, as the owner, would not be covered yourself; therefore it is wise to make certain that your personal medical policy will cover you.

5. *Disability insurance* will pay up to sixty percent of your gross income if you can't work for any length of time because of an injury or illness. This can also be made available to employees on an optional basis.

6. *Business overhead protection* is the business equivalent of disability insurance. If you can't be actively involved in the

running of the business due to a disability, this policy will pay such expenses as rent and utilities to help keep it going in your absence.

7. *Key person insurance* will provide a death benefit to the business if you or a key employee dies suddenly and this event directly affects the financial stability of the company.

8. *Car insurance* will be a necessity if you have a car or truck used exclusively for business travel or needs. Other employees who use these vehicles should be included in the policy coverage.

When setting up your business, be sure to go to a trusted adviser to determine what insurance coverage you are most likely to need. Then buy it. Lack of adequate insurance in the event of a calamity can create an even bigger calamity for your business!

38

WHEN THE BUSINESS *ISN'T* PERFORMING THE WAY YOU WANT

Even the most careful and exact planning can't guarantee that everything will go exactly the way you want it to. Frequently, circumstances beyond an owner's control may play a part in the success or failure of a business. Sometimes, however, those circumstances may be within our control. Though there are many elements to running a business, and it's difficult to oversee all aspects and ensure that everything will go according to plan, sometimes the plan was wrong to begin with and needs revising.

Whatever the case, the trick is to prepare yourself and be alert for signs of trouble before it seriously affects your profits.

Those warning signs can get lost in the maze of work and obligations that you have to deal with every day. They're there, all around you, but in your preoccupation with meetings and selling and attending to masses of paperwork, you can easily miss them—they're that subtle. For instance, take a look at your current office situation. Are your employees happy, or does there seem to be a lot of disgruntlement? Is there a lot of turnover, perhaps too much, and do you have trouble hiring new employees? Are you communicating well with your people, or does there frequently seem to be a wall between you and them? Indeed, can you detect any sign of an us-versus-them mentality within your organization? Is there genuine teamwork taking place, or is everyone just passing the ball off to someone else? Do your employees go the extra mile when asked (or even when not asked), or do they empty out of the office at five on the dot?

Most important, are your employees clear about the company's mission and their role in it? If not, then it's time to review the mission and clarify it—both for them and for yourself. If your workers seem apathetic and care little about the company or its future, then your business is in trouble.

Your employees are the lifeblood of your organization. If the business isn't performing the way you want it to, then that may mean your people are not performing the way you want them to. And if that's the case, you can point the finger at only one person—yourself. I've already talked quite a bit about hiring and dealing with a staff. One of the most important things to remember is that you must give them as much respect as you expect them to give you. The concept of teamwork works both ways. If your employees aren't truly involved in the company—if they are treated like drones and shown no respect for their intelligence or abilities—then they are less likely to give you the results you want. The state of your organizational culture is a pretty good indication of the state of your business. If one is suffering, so will the other.

To get around this problem, get out among your employees and listen. Talk to all your staff, at every level of the organization. Ask questions, solicit their input, and really, really listen. There are several benefits that will come from this, chief among them, your employees will know that you really care about what they have to say and will be more inclined to go that extra mile for you as a result. Remember, you get back what you give out.

But listening has another benefit, as well: You may learn something you didn't know or realize previously, and it may give you insight into what is wrong with the company and how to turn it around. Indeed, somebody on your staff may have just the solution for your business, a solution not even the brightest of your executives and managers may have envisioned. Answers can be found in what may seem to be the unlikeliest of places. Those in the trenches of a business are closest to the action and may have a clearer idea of what's really going on than the generals behind the lines.

So get out there and listen to your employees, not just when times get bad, but at all times. Being tuned in to what they're thinking and feeling can give you the insight you need to keep your business afloat. It also helps to encourage high morale and instill the sense of a shared purpose with your staff. Consistently review and reaffirm your company's mission and its goals with your employees. The more tuned in they are to you—and the more tuned in you are to them—the better off everybody will be.

Another indicator is your customers. How are they regarding you these days? Is there a high level of satisfaction, or have you noticed an increase in customer complaints? How are you and your company perceived in the marketplace? Do you maintain honest and fair prices and policies, or do you favor some customers at the expense of others? Do you feel your customers respect and trust you, or is there often an adversarial relationship between you and them? Are you aware of what your company's reputation is, good or bad? A reputation as a good, solid, trustworthy company will pay off in the end—handsomely. No matter how big your company grows, you always have to focus attention on your customers—what they need, what they want, what they're not getting now.

As with your employees, it will be helpful to you and beneficial to the company if you get out and listen to what the customers have to say about your product or service and what improvements might be made. Take periodic surveys to rate customer-satisfaction levels. If you see those levels dipping, it's time to take some action. In the same regard, you might also gain some valuable insight from your customers into what specifically is going wrong in terms of your product or your service and what corrective action might be taken that would reduce the complaints or win back lost clientele.

Another clue to potential trouble is an obvious one: the state of your finances. How stable are they? How is your cash flow? Is it strong enough to support all areas of your business? If not, what area is suffering or will require sacrifice on your part?

It may be tempting to ignore warning signs. You're busy, you have a lot on your mind, you don't think you have the time to talk to employees and customers that way, and so on. Yet the subtlest of warning signs can indicate big trouble. Act now, before it's too late. Find out where the problems are and make the changes you need to make.

There's an old Ukrainian saying that applies here: If you don't change what you're doing, nothing different happens!

39

WHEN THE BUSINESS *IS* PERFORMING THE WAY YOU WANT

Oh, how easy it is to become complacent! Things are going so smoothly, the business is practically running itself. Revenues are high, employee turnover is low, crises almost never arise, and the whole picture seems absolutely hunky-dory, doesn't it? You seem to have found the perfect formula, so you may as well stick with it. "If it ain't broke, don't fix it"— right?

Wrong! One of the worst things you can do when owning a business is to become too self-confident when things are going well. Success has hidden dangers built into it. It's possible to become profitable in the short term and still lose money in the long run because you didn't plan well enough for possible outcomes or unexpected crises. You also risk being caught unprepared when you fail to plan for the changes that will inevitably occur in the marketplace and in rapidly developing technology.

Let's say you based your business on a single great idea

that responded to a need in the current American culture. You took out a patent and launched this idea and were met with instant sales and overwhelming approval. "No home should be without the Super Duper Widget" was your motto, and the public seemed to agree. They liked it, they bought it, they raved about it to their friends. It worked so well that it seemed to sell itself, and you had that patent in your pocket. "If it ain't broke, don't fix it," you said to yourself, so you continued merrily along, turning out Super Duper Widgets easily and complacently.

Meanwhile, your competitors have been doing their homework and have figured out how to make a similar product that's also better and even more suited to customer needs—and it costs less, too. Since you have done nothing yourself in the way of market research, you're taken by surprise when the new Widget knockoffs take the public by storm. Next thing you know, your sales are dipping, and you have to struggle to catch up with the competition. By the time you come out with your New and Improved Super Duper Widget, it's too late. One of your competitor's models has now become the industry standard, and you are just one of a crowd, with nothing to single you out—except, perhaps, a lot of excess inventory that will never sell.

That is just one example of what might happen if you don't do your homework carefully and don't prepare for changes in the marketplace. And these changes are happening at a much more rapid pace than they ever were. Tastes change, styles change, people change. It's just a fact of life. Today's success story can very quickly become yesterday's fad, and if you can't anticipate what customers are likely to want and need today and in the future, then you can probably expect to be included in one of those "Whatever happened to—" conversations you so often hear at parties.

The moral of this story is: Don't cling too much to old ideas, or you'll simply end up with a lot of old inventory. What works now won't necessarily work in the future. The minute your new product or service is launched, somebody will be out there trying to think of ways to make it bigger, better, faster, more convenient, less expensive, and so on. Thus, a large part of your job is to beat your competitors to the punch!

It's not just your competitors that you have to look out for. It's also the economy. At both a national and a local level, the economy can change with much the same rapidity and unpredictability as the public's tastes. When this happens, it's even more difficult to anticipate what customers may or may not want to buy. In a recession, most people are likely to spend less, especially if jobs are lost or salaries are frozen. Even those who have not been adversely affected are likely to restrain their spending, just in case they are the next ones to be hit. More often than not, this has a domino effect: Customers buy less, so retailers buy less, so wholesalers and distributors buy less, so you're left holding the inventory.

These days, predicting which way the economy is going to turn seems to have become more of an art than a science. But you better your chances for staying alive if you stay on top of market and economic trends and pay attention to what the experts have to say, then plan accordingly. Unless your product or service is guaranteed to become permanently embedded in the culture—and few things do—you'd better be prepared for the economic downturns.

The impact of politics is another aspect of business to watch out for. On both a national and a local level, legislators are always doing something that affects small businesses— beneficially or detrimentally. It may be new laws that require you to pay more in taxes or benefits to your employees; or it may be new zoning that permits the building of a shopping mall that will likely take business away from your small store; or it may be that you are forced to vacate your premises because some developer with a politician in his or her pocket is going to raze the entire block; or it may be that the bigger business with the greater political influence got the jump on you and stole away the contract you felt was yours.

If you set up a business, you should be aware of what is

going on around you politically. Local and national events and legislation are always likely to have some effect, great or small, on what you are trying to accomplish. It is to your advantage not to be caught by surprise. Stay on top of the latest news, especially locally, in order to know what is going on that may affect your business.

40

REDEFINING YOUR ROLE

Growth inevitably brings change. When you start your business, you will more than likely wear all the various hats needed to oversee just about all aspects of your business. You are CEO, CFO, sales manager, warehouse manager, office manager, personnel supervisor, accountant, and clerk, all rolled into one concentrated package. But with each step toward achieving your goals and each plateau of success that you reach, your business will change and become more complicated. In two years' time, you probably won't be doing the same things that you're doing now—it just won't be feasible. Your role in the company will change out of necessity. You knew how to define that role when you were starting up. Now you need to learn how to redefine it so that you and the company can grow and succeed comfortably, as a well-oiled unit.

What sort of changes are in store for you? For starters, there's the obvious development: As your business expands, it will become increasingly impossible for you to carry the full workload yourself. You will need to free yourself from clerical details and from tasks not to your liking or that don't fit your talents in order to focus on those larger matters requiring your greater attention. This will mean hiring the people you need (as you can afford them) to assume some of the hats you've been wearing and some of the ones that may have been created as a result of your expansion.

Probably the most important aspect of your changing role is that of team leader. When it was just you and one or two other people, you probably had a sense of family and real teamwork. But as you grow and take on new employees and greater responsibilities, you may become more distant from those "in the trenches." The duties that remove you from the nitty-gritty grunt work also remove you in many ways from the people now doing that work. Like it or not, an invisible line forms: You are management; they are the workers. But that line can be crossed. As owner of your organization, you are their leader. And as their leader, it is up to you to instill that sense of family and teamwork that was a big part of the company in its earliest days. Just because your company grows doesn't mean you have to become impersonal. If anything, you need that personal touch more than ever to provide inspiration and motivation for the people you have working for you. And if you're smart, you'll also keep your employees involved in the business as much as possible.

Earlier, we discussed the importance of listening to your employees as it relates to the times when your company is in trouble. It is just as important to listen when your company is successful. Giving employees a chance to express ideas and suggestions and to see their thoughts and concerns taken seriously, not only enhances morale and teamwork, but can lead to insights that result in large increases in your company's profitability. Your ideas and effort got your business off the ground, but you can't continue to rely solely on your own fuel. You need the fuel that your employees can provide in order to keep it in the air and soaring ever higher.

41

SELLING YOUR BUSINESS

When the time comes to sell the business, you'll know it. Just as you once knew that you wanted to go into business for yourself, so you will know when you want to get out. I've heard any number of reasons why an owner has decided it's time to sell. Maybe you fall into one of the following categories.

You're not having fun anymore. The challenge and the joy have gone out of your work. Instead there's a feeling of drudgery and resentment because the business is taking up so much of your time—time you'd rather be spending with your family or on other interests.

You're tired and bored. You've put a lot of time and energy into the business for years, and it no longer holds the interest and excitement that it once did for you. The days have become a drag, and you're more inclined to go play a round of golf than to go into the office. You're ready to make a change.

You've done all you can or care to do with this business. Now you want to move on to new opportunities and challenges.

You're overwhelmed. The company has become too big for you to handle. You had a flair for the business earlier, but now you wonder whether you're out of your depth.

You're ready to retire. You've worked all your life, and you can afford to do it. It's time to leave the world of work behind you and pursue other dreams—like that round-the-world trip you've been wanting to take for years.

You're short of cash. For whatever reason, you need money, and selling the business is your only viable method of getting it.

You're on to something. You've sensed change in the economic winds, and you want to get out while you're still ahead of the game.

You're faced with a personal crisis. Illness or accident— yours or a family member's—or some other situation requires you to focus most or all of your attention elsewhere.

You're made an offer you can't refuse. Your business is doing so well that a larger corporation now wants to snap you up. The financial incentives are too good to pass up. You may even be kept on to run the company as president or CEO.

Experts agree that the primary reason most people choose to sell their business is loss of interest and motivation. When it's no longer a joy for you to get up each morning and see what the day has to offer you, then it's probably time to consider selling. Those same experts also advise that it's best to be prepared for the possibility of selling from the very day that you open. For whether you sell it or exit your business by some other means, the likelihood is that you will leave it sooner or later. Anticipating that possibility will prompt you to keep your business in fine form and ready for the day when you do hand it over to somebody else.

As with every other aspect of running a business, there is a certain amount of prep work to do before you actually sell it.

No matter how well you keep your books in order, for example, they may still need to be reviewed and cleaned up—particularly the balance sheet and the profit-and-loss statement. Any nonoperating assets that will not be included in the sale of the business should be moved off the books, and any of your income that has not been reported should be moved on to them.

You should also have your business plan thoroughly up-to-date. This can and will be an important tool in the selling of your business. You will need to revise it somewhat so that it can serve as a selling memorandum. It is this memorandum that will be a potential buyer's first introduction to your company. You will need to include in it a thorough history of your company and a description of its products/services, as well as the market in which you operate, your position in that market, and your strengths. You should emphasize those things that make your company unique and provide a complete and accurate description of its marketing, manufacturing, management, personnel, and finances. The financial section should include statements for the last three years, as well as comparative analyses of results with budgets and any auditors' reports. You should also provide projections of earnings for the next three to five years.

Once you have thoroughly prepared your selling memorandum, you must turn your attention to the harder part of the prep work—valuing your business. This is a necessary step to take prior to putting your business on the market and also a very difficult one, as no two businesses can ever be considered exactly alike. You probably launched your business in the first place because you had a unique idea, and it's that uniqueness that sets you apart from other businesses. Your valuation will depend on a large number of elements, but most of all, it will depend on your cash flow—that is, your business's ability to generate profits consistently.

The valuation will determine the price you're going to ask for your business, so it should be undertaken with care and consideration, whether you do it alone or with the assistance of an appraiser. The following points should be considered:

- an analysis of your products or services: their strengths and weaknesses, as well as their position in the market and reputation in the industry
- your business's current and estimated future market share
- your business's product-development capabilities
- trends in the market and in the industry
- potential changes in relevant technology
- your competitors and their products/services
- marketing and sales for your business, including current distribution methods and pricing strategies
- the manufacturing of your product: materials, labor, overhead, operations, product costs, inventory, and the state of the facilities
- your business's finances: present and future working capital, investment requirements, and analysis of present and future profitability (financial projections)
- your business's management: who is currently on board, how easily they could be replaced if they left unexpectedly, and present and future personnel requirements
- the salaries and benefits provided by your company

A thorough analysis of your business will not only assist in its valuation, but may also identify areas for improvement that if fixed quickly will make a higher asking price possible.

Valuation is an incredibly complicated topic, one that you will probably need help with. *Don't assume that you can determine the final selling price of your business on your own!* Consider enlisting the help of a professional—perhaps a retired businessperson in your area—in establishing the market price. Contact the Service Corps of Retired Executives for details on tracking down a retired pro who can help you in this area.

Once the valuation is done, you're ready to sell. But should you do it yourself? The experts say, "Don't!" Selling a business is not like selling a car, or even a house. No matter how savvy you are, there are too many complexities involved in the sale of a business, not to mention tremendous hassles dealing with phone calls and meetings and paperwork for which you have no preparation or skills. Finding the right buyer may be overwhelming and well beyond your capabilities. So you should once again turn to a professional—a business broker.

Like a real estate agent, a business broker is able to do all the dirty work for you and can screen potential buyers, thus matching the right buyer to your business with greater ease than you could if you went searching for one on your own. Be sure, however, to conduct your own thorough search for the right business broker for you. It's best to go with a specialist who has had sufficient experience in your particular field to be able to represent you honestly and fairly. If you have any difficulty finding such a broker, try locating one that has been designated as a certified business intermediary. You might also try the International Business Brokers Association for assistance.

One of the functions a broker can serve is to keep the sale of your business confidential. If you have employees to consider, it would serve no purpose to get them into a state of anxiety over their job security by letting them know you have put the business up for sale. So above and beyond all else, stay mum about what you're doing until the deal has gone through and you have something concrete you can tell your staff.

When do you know you have the right buyer? If the broker has done his or her job well, the answer will be delivered to your doorstep. Nevertheless, you should make sure that your broker has taken certain things into consideration, the details of which can be provided to you. For instance: What are the prospective buyer's credentials? What is his experience? What is her track record? Has his credit history been thoroughly investigated? Does she have a solid reputation for integrity and trustworthiness? Why does he or she want to buy your business?

Before selling your business, you need to make absolutely

certain that you are putting it into the right hands; so be sure all the homework has been done and you have all the facts about your potential buyer before closing the deal. Something may very well turn up that will make you realize this is not the right buyer for you. What you want is a new owner whose goals and business philosophy match your own as closely as possible. Only then can you feel truly secure in passing over the keys to the company.

Remember, the tax issues and legal implications of the sale of your businesss can be truly awesome in scale. Make sure you've secured the right professional advice before you sign on the dotted line.

A few words on retirement are also in order here. The same reasons that may apply to your decision to sell your business may also apply to your decision to retire, although there may also be factors such as advancing age to consider. Your reasons are, of course, entirely personal, but whatever they are, when the time to bow out is upon you, you have two major considerations: What do you do about the business, and what are you going to do for yourself?

Anticipating and planning for your retirement is something that can and should be done from early on in your working career, not just when you're getting ready to sell a business. Obviously, you'll need to build up your savings and set up a retirement plan for yourself, even if you decide not to sell your company—unless you plan on working forever. It's also a good idea to establish a retirement date as a goal to shoot for, even if it's not going to materialize for some time. This will give you ample opportunity to start your preparations now and have everything in readiness, both financially and spiritually, by the time the appointed date rolls around. You can and should work with a certified financial planner to determine how much money you're going to need at the time of your retirement and how you are going to go about saving and investing to meet your retirement goals.

42

SUCCESSFUL EXIT STRATEGIES

There are a number of reasons why you're going to need a good exit strategy. If you're lucky, your business may have become so successful that you're now ready to sell it and cruise the Caribbean. After all, you've worked hard all those years—now you're ready to take it easy! Or perhaps your motivation has changed; you may have grown bored with your business and want to seek out new challenges for yourself. However, there's a good chance that you decide to sell because things are simply not going the way you thought they would and it's become too much of a struggle to maintain your business. Nobody really likes to admit defeat, but sometimes it's necessary to call it a day and move on.

Whatever your motivation may be, when it is indeed time to call it quits, you have to be prepared to make as graceful and cost-effective an exit as possible. And for that you need a good strategy.

The strategy that will work best for you will depend on

your situation. Although your situation will be unique, you should know that there are four basic methods that you can employ to get out of your business, and the particular exit strategy you choose will probably depend on which of these methods you employ.

One method is to *transfer the ownership of the company,* usually to a family member. This is possibly the most appealing to you, especially if yours is a family-run business in the first place. However, there are a few risks involved that you should take into consideration. One is the risk you take when you receive no financial remuneration. You have to be absolutely certain before you do this that you are well set financially and will continue to live comfortably. There is also the risk of having it all backfire on you. Involving family means possibly harming the ties that bind you together. Disagreements, failure to set up a working structure to which all can agree, deciding who gets what—these can all affect your relationship with your family and theirs with each other. Careful planning and assurance that all will agree to abide by the terms you set are absolute necessities when you turn your business over to family members.

The better way to go may be to *sell your interest in the company to another person or persons*—say, your partner or one or more of your employees. This has numerous advantages, chief among them your ability to handpick and groom your successor. You may, for instance, choose a younger person to buy into ownership in your company while you're still working, thus giving him or her the opportunity to learn the business while you are still around to offer guidance and advice, as well as to determine whether this person has what it takes to assume leadership. Injecting fresh blood also brings vitality into your business and keeps it fresh for future development. Finally, when you know you are putting the business in the hands of somebody who is experienced, understands what it needs, and shares your vision for the company, this eases the process of turning it over.

Your third option is to *sell outright to another nonfamily individual or individuals,* a subject discussed earlier in this book. The inherent problem of this option is the unknowns involved in selling to somebody you don't know. How does his or her style fit with your business? How will he or she be perceived by your employees and customers? You may have a transition period during which you will have to continue working for the company for a specified time, until the transfer of the ownership is completed to everybody's satisfaction—which only delays your retirement.

Finally, you may choose to *liquidate your assets.* This can be an option if there is no one to buy or take over your business or if you simply feel that it has run its course and has no real future. This is a low-risk way to go. You simply sell everything off, finish collecting on your receivables, pay off your bills, and hold on to what's left at the end. However, this option doesn't give you the satisfaction of leaving some sort of legacy to all the hard work and dedication that you put into the business over the years.

EPILOGUE

You've reached the end of this book—but this is only the beginning for you.

As you pursue your dream of *making it on your own*, I'd like you to remember that the most important part of building any business is commitment. Commitment takes many forms: commitment to your customers, commitment to your highest ethical standards, commitment to your employees, commitment to the power of an idea, and commitment to build a life that makes sense for you. All of these are commitments that should work together in the company you build, and as I close this book, I offer you the best closing wish any entrepreneur could ask for: May all your commitments be rewarded with abundance and happiness.

Please share your thoughts on the ideas and principles in this book with me. I'm eager to hear your reactions to the advice contained here—and to find out what worked for you (and what didn't) in this program. Write me at:

DEI Management Group, Inc.
888 Seventh Avenue (9th fl.)
New York, NY 10106

Good luck!

APPENDIX A
Your Formal Business Plan

Your formal business plan is a tool, one that will help you set your strategy and (perhaps just as important) increase the chances of your securing funding from banks or other financial institutions.

There is no right way and no wrong way to do business. There is only the way that works best for you. Once you know what you want, you have to figure out your best route for getting there.

This means mapping out a strategy that will provide the guidance you need to reach your destination. A business plan provides the structure you need to determine the all-important question of where you're headed and how you'll get there. Your business plan will not be written overnight. In fact, you can expect to take several months to put it together in a cohesive, working form that clearly articulates your goals and how they will be achieved.

A good business plan should have five key components:

1. The statement of purpose (one page) should state the name and location of your business, as well as its structure and mission. If your business plan is to be used to attract investors, this statement should also provide a clear indication of how much money is needed for your purposes, what the return may be on any investment, and the anticipated length of time for payback.

2. Your organizational plan should provide a concise summary of every aspect of your business, from management down to distribution. You should describe your organizational and legal structure, your personnel, your finances, and your objectives at every level.

3. Your marketing plan should describe the market you are targeting; the demand for your product, service, or solution within that market; the competition; and how you intend to distribute your product or service. You also need to describe industry trends, especially as they affect your pricing, and note what promotional methods you intend to use.

4. Your financial statement should detail how much money will be needed to achieve your goals and where that money will come from. Other areas to be covered include a cash-flow statement, a three-year income projection, a balance sheet listing current and fixed assets, and an assessment of all liabilities. In addition, you should provide an analysis of how long it will take before you turn a profit (the break-even point), as well as the company's net worth.

5. Finally, your management-team biographies should provide the personal details on you and any members of your management team—that is, degrees, work experience, skills, role in the company hierarchy, and financial interest.

Fortunately there is plenty of information and assistance available to help you structure your business plan. In addition to exploring the resources available via the Internet, you might want to enlist the aid of a business counselor through the local Small Business Administration office or look for workshops geared to writing business plans, which are often held at local colleges. The sponsors of these workshops are usually available to offer guidance and assistance and can also help to steer the entrepreneur to an appropriate lending institution.

There are also excellent software packages on the market that will help you to assemble a solid, effective business plan, as well as cash-flow analyses and financial projections. Some typical packages are Business Plan Pro, Plan Write, and the most popular, BizPlan Builder. However, be careful. The software can't write your plan for you! The program will only ensure that you don't omit any crucial elements to a business plan. It will never provide the personalized touch that distinguishes your business plan from all the others out there (and impresses bankers and investors). Use the software sparingly to give you a foundation for your own, personalized final plan.

In that same vein, one possible Internet resource is the free on-line guide offered by American Express at www.americanexpress.com/smallbusiness/resource. You should also check out the fine advice available through the Small Business Administration's Web site at www.sba.gov. But once again, use caution when applying any guide to your own plan. Remember, you want your plan to stand out from the crowd, not blend in with all the others!

Once your business plan is written and you begin to use it to set goals and sales quotas, there are four basic rules to keep in mind:

1. If you're preparing the plan as part of a presentation to a lending institution or investor, *ask about required elements ahead of time* and then include them. Don't let this book—or any other book—tell you what the "right" format is. What your audience wants to see is the "right" format.

2. *Your business plan does not amount to the Ten Commandments.* It can and should be reviewed periodically and modified as needed. Check your progress as you go along. How well are you meeting the goals you set for the business? Are sales less or greater than anticipated? Have you come across new markets that can be incorporated into your plan?

What new developments in the industry are affecting your product or service? There are numerous factors that will affect how your business plan works or doesn't work. You have to stay on top of current trends and happenings to ensure that your plan keeps pace with the times and with the industry.

3. *Have a backup plan ready in case your initial plan fails.* No one is omniscient. However certain we may be that our plan will succeed, there may still be circumstances that we didn't anticipate that foil our efforts. If this happens to you, you have two options: You can quit, or you can go to Plan B. Having an alternative ready, just in case, gives you something to fall back on, a second chance to make good.

4. When using your plan as a basis for a proposal to a bank or investor, remember that *neatness counts!* The sharper your plan looks on paper, the more care and attention you display in researching or assembling it, the more rigorously you check it for numerical or typographical errors, the greater your chance of success.

APPENDIX B
Interview Questions You Can Use to Evaluate Candidates for Employment

1. Tell me about yourself.
2. What's your greatest strength?
3. What's your greatest weakness?
4. What do you like least about your current boss? (Note: An applicant with a long litany of grievances against a current employer may turn out to be a real headache for you down the line.)
5. Why should I hire you for this position?
6. Give me an example of a time you pitched in, in an area outside of your formal job description.
7. Whom do you most admire? Why?
8. What salary level are you looking for?
9. What kinds of people do you find it easiest to work with?
10. What kinds of people do you find it hardest to work with?
11. What would you like to see yourself doing five years from now?
12. Do you think you would have difficulty adapting to an environment like this one? Why or why not?

ACKNOWLEDGMENTS

Any undertaking, such as writing a book, is a collaborative effort. It requires the assistance and guidance of many people to mold and develop the concepts into what will become the final work. For nearly thirty years I have been given the opportunity to work with many fine and dedicated individuals. For this project I would especially like to thank Brandon Toropov for his unending efforts in assembling the manuscript. Other individuals who continually provided encouragement include Lynne Einleger, Steve Bookbinder, Michele Reisner, Sheila Salera, Kim Bradford, Nancy Bellard, Greg Hudson, Kathy Gantz, Scott Buckler, and Sean Kilbride. A special note of appreciation has to be paid to Denise Lopresti, who, for lack of a better work, shepherded this book from its first outline to its completion. And, of course, without Anne's continuing support, which began twenty-five years ago, none of these would have happened. Also, special thanks go to Danielle and Jennifer.

ABOUT THE AUTHOR

Stephan Schiffman is the founder and president of DEI Management Group, one of the nation's leading sales training and consulting firms. His clients include AT&T, Motorola, and Aetna/U.S. Healthcare. He is the author of twelve books, including *Cold Calling Techniques (That Really Work)*—which has sold more than 100,000 copies—and *The 25 Sales Habits of Highly Successful Salespeople*. He has also recorded several audiotapes, including *Getting Through, High-Efficiency Selling*, and *25 Sales Secrets*.